AMERICAN VOICES FROM

The Opening of the West

AMERICAN VOICES FROM

The Opening of the West

Rebecca Stefoff

BENCHMARK BOOKS

MARSHALL CAVENDISH
NEW YORK

Benchmark Books
Marshall Cavendish
99 White Plains Road
Tarrytown, New York 10591-9001
www.marshallcavendish.com

Text copyright © 2003 by Marshall Cavendish Corporation
Map © 2003 by Marshall Cavendish Corporation
Maps by Laszlo Kubinyi

Stefoff, Rebecca, 1951–
The opening of the West / by Rebecca Stefoff.
p. cm. — (American voices from—)
Summary: Presents the history of the westward expansion of the United States in the eighteenth and nineteenth centuries through excerpts from letters, newspaper articles, journal entries, and laws of the time. Includes bibliographical references and index.
ISBN 0-7614-1201-8
1. West (U.S.)—History—Juvenile literature. 2. West (U.S.)—History—Sources—Juvenile literature. 3. Pioneers—West (U.S.) —History—Juvenile literature. 4. Pioneers—West (U.S.)—History—Sources—Juvenile literature. 5. Frontier and pioneer life—West (U.S.)—Juvenile literature. 6. Frontier and pioneer life—West (U.S.)—Sources—Juvenile literature. 7. United States—Territorial expansion—Juvenile literature. [1. West (U.S.)—History. 2. Frontier and pioneer life—West (U.S.) 3. United states—Territorial expansion.] I. Title. II. Series.
F591 .S8223 2002   978'.02—dc21
2001008681
Printed in Italy
1 3 5 6 4 2

Series design and composition by Anne Scatto / PIXEL PRESS
Photo Research by Anne Burns Images

Cover Photo: Bridgeman Art Library/Christie's Images
The photographs in this book are used by permission and through the courtesy of:
Bridgeman Art Library: p.ii, 12/Index; xix/Reynolds Museum, Winston Salem, NC; xx/Kennedy Galleries
North Wind Pictures: p. viii, 18, 19, 55, 79, 81, 88
Colorado Historical Society: p. xi
Denver Public Library: p. xii, 28, 44
Art Resource: p.xiv/Giraudon
New York Public Library: p. 14
The Granger Collection: p. 5, 65
C.M.Russell Museum: p. 11
Archive Photos: p. 22, 98; 38, 72/Hulton Getty
John Powell National Archives: p. 24
Superstock: p. 27/Metropolitan Museum of Art & Bridgeman Art Library; 74/Christie's Images; 87/A&F Pears Ltd., London
Library of Congress: p.33
Oregon Historical Society: p. 40, 56, 77
Museum of Church History and Art: p. 49, 52, 59(top & bottom),66, 100 (top right and bottom left) 101(bottom left and right)
Western History Collections, University of Oaklahoma Libraries: p. 90, 96
U.S. Post Office: p. 100(top left), 101(top)

ON THE COVER: American illustrator Howard Pyle portrayed New England settlers entering the Ohio River Valley as both humble and heroic—ordinary men and women at an extraordinary moment in history.

ON THE TITLE PAGE: The opening of the West brought white scouts and settlers into the last places that Native Americans still held as their own. The contacts that resulted were sometimes peaceful and sometimes violent, but they always led to the loss of Indian lands.

Acknowledgments

The author is grateful to the staff of the Oregon History Center, Portland, Oregon; the End of the Trail Interpretive Center, Oregon City, Oregon; and the History Department of the Multnomah County Library, Oregon.

Two extracts from the papers of Thomas Jefferson, in *The Papers of Thomas Jefferson,* ed. Julian Boyd. Princeton: Princeton University Press, 1950. Reprinted by permission of Princeton University Press.

Extract from the journal of Zebulon Pike, in *The Journals of Zebulon Montgomery Pike,* ed. Donald Jackson. Norman: University of Oklahoma Press, 1966. Reprinted by permission of the University of Oklahoma Press.

Extract from the report of John C. Frémont, in *Fremont's Greatest Western Exploration, Volume 1: The Dalles to Pyramid Lake,* ed. John L. Stewart. Vancouver, WA: SET, Inc., 1999. Reprinted by permission of John L. Stewart and SET, Inc.

Two extracts from the memoir of Martha Gay Masterson, in *One Woman's West,* ed. Lois Barton. Eugene, OR: Spencer Butte Press, 1986. Reprinted by permission of Lois Barton and Spencer Butte Press.

Numaga's speech, in *Gunfighters, Highwaymen, and Vigilantes: Violence on the Frontier,* by Roger McGrath. Berkeley: University of California Press, 1984. Reprinted by permission of the University of California Press.

Chief Joseph's speech, in *Hear Me, My Chiefs,* by Lucullus Virgil McWhorter. Caldwell, ID: Caxton, 1952. Reprinted by permission of Scott Gibson and Caxton Printers.

Contents

Grouse
are
about
short
and eye.
Cock
Cock
which
on the
and
-hood
Mountains
to the Mountain
the Columbia
the great falls
they go in large
or singularly

the feathers about its head
pointed and stiff some hairs
the base of the beak. feathers
fine and stiff about the ears.
This is a faint likeness of the
of the Plains or Heath
the first of those four
we met with was
Mysoure below
in the neighbour
of the Rocky
and from
which pass
between
and Rapids
Gorge
and
was

hide hide remarkably close when pursued.
short flights &c.
The large Black & White Pheasant is peculiar
to that portion of the Rocky Mountains watered by
the Columbia River. at least we did not see them untill
we reached the waters of that river, nor since we have
left those Mountains. they are about the size of a
well grown hen. the contour of the bird is much
that of the reddish brown Pheasant common to
our country. the tail is proportionably as long and is
composed of 18 feathers of equal length. of a uniform
dark brown tiped with black. the feathers of the
body are of a dark brown black and white. the black

About Primary Sources

What Is a Primary Source?

In the pages that follow, you will be hearing many different "voices" from a special time in America's past. Some of the selections are long while others are short. You'll find many easy to understand at first reading, but some may require several readings. All the selections have one thing in common, however. They are primary sources. This is the name historians give to the bits and pieces of information that make up the record of human existence. Primary sources are important to us because they are the very essence, the core material for all historical investigation. You can call them "history" itself.

Primary sources *are* evidence; they give historians the all-important clues they need to understand the past. Perhaps you have read a detective story in which a sleuth must solve a mystery by piecing

OPPOSITE: **One of the most famous and important primary sources in the history of the American West is the diary kept by explorer William Clark on his 1804–1806 journey to the Pacific coast and back. Clark sketched many things he saw, including this bird encountered on the Great Plains.**

together bits of evidence he or she uncovers. The detective makes deductions, or educated guesses based on the evidence, and solves the mystery once all the deductions point in a certain direction. Historians work in much the same way. Like detectives, historians analyze the data by careful reading and rereading. After much analysis, historians draw conclusions about an event, a person, or an entire era. Historians may analyze the same evidence and come to different conclusions. This is why there is often sharp disagreement about an event.

Primary sources are also called *documents*—a rather dry word to describe what can be just about anything: an official speech by a government leader, an old map, an act of Congress, a letter worn out from too much handling, an entry hastily scrawled into a diary, a detailed newspaper account of a tragic event, a funny or sad song, a colorful poster, a cartoon, a faded photograph, or someone's eloquent remembrance captured on tape or film.

By examining the following primary sources, you, the reader, will be taking on the role of historian. Here is your chance to immerse yourself in an exciting era of American history—the opening of the West. You'll come to know the voices of the men and women who explored and settled America's great frontier. You'll read the words of Native Americans and pioneers, miners and mountain men, homemakers and homesteaders.

Our language has changed since those early days. People were more formal in the way they wrote. Their everyday vocabulary contained many words that will be unfamiliar to someone living in this century. Sometimes they spelled words differently, too.

Don't be discouraged! Trying to figure out language is exactly the kind of work a historian does. Like a historian, when your work is done, you will have a deeper, more meaningful understanding of the past.

How to Read a Primary Source

Each document in this book deals with the opening of the American West. Some of the documents are from government archives such as the Library of Congress. Others are from the official papers of major figures in American history. Many of the documents are taken from the letters and diaries that ordinary people wrote. All of the documents, major and minor, help us to understand what it was like to be part of the great movement west.

A medal made to commemorate the life of explorer Zebulon Montgomery Pike. While following the Arkansas River in 1806, Pike sighted the tall peak in the Rocky Mountains that now bears his name. Some people think his mission was more about spying than exploring.

As you read each document, ask yourself some basic but important questions. Who is writing? Who is the writer's audience? What is the writer's point of view? What is he or she trying

This cottage was built by Dr. D.W. King of Empire, Colorado in the spring of 1861. My daughter Nellie Augusta was born here Feb. 10th 1862. My son George H. King was born here Nov. 26th 1863. Noted men who were guests: Hon. Bayard Taylor, Secretary of State, — Hon. J.B. Chaffee. — Capt. C.M. Tyler. — N.K. Smith. — Col. Levenworth. — Sam Tappan. — Rocky Mountain Reno, — Governor Evans, Jim Bridger, old Rocky Mountain Scout, my father's friend in 1834. — Dr. Cook of Smithsonian Institution, Washington, D. C.

Vanna S. King

Officials and scholars are not the only historians. Personal remembrances, such as this note attached to an old photograph of a pioneer cabin, are primary sources woven into the fabric of history.

to tell that audience? Is the message clearly expressed or is it implied, that is, stated indirectly? What words does the writer use to convey his or her message? Are the words emotion filled or objective in tone? If you are looking at a photograph, examine it carefully, taking in all the details. Where do you think it was taken? What's happening in the foreground? In the background? Is it posed? Or is it an action shot? How can you tell? Who do you think took the picture? What is its purpose? These are questions that help you think critically about a document.

Some tools have been included with the documents to help you in your historical investigations. Unusual words have been listed and defined near some selections. Thought-provoking questions follow many of the documents. They help focus your reading so you get the most out of the document. As you read each selection, you'll probably come up with many questions of your own. That's great! The work of a historian always leads to many, many questions. Some can be answered, others cannot and require further investigation.

In the mid-nineteenth century, French artist Jean Antoine Gudin painted this scene of Jacques Cartier entering the Saint Lawrence River in 1535. By highlighting the vast landscape and the Native Americans rather than the explorer, the artist emphasized the challenges faced by a handful of lonely Europeans in an alien land.

Introduction

THE WAY WEST

People came to North America from many directions. The first of them to arrive came from Asia. Scientists do not yet know exactly when these prehistoric humans first reached North America, but it was sometime before 11,000 years ago. In those years the water level of the world's oceans was lower than it is today. What is now the bottom of the Bering Strait, part of the North Pacific Ocean, was above sea level. Huge, shaggy, elephant-like mammoths, herds of grazing reindeer, and other game animals crossed this land bridge from northeastern Asia to western Alaska. Human hunters followed them, probably in several slow waves of migration, before the ice melted and the waters rose, drowning the land bridge. These people, and then their children and grandchildren, began to spread out through the Americas. Their descendants, the Native Americans, later had a tragic role in the opening of the American West.

Thousands of years after people from Asia reached the Americas, Europeans began to arrive. Around A.D. 1000 Viking seafarers, originally from northern Europe, briefly touched the east coast of what is now Canada. They landed at a place they called Vinland, probably on the coast of Newfoundland Island. Viking legends tell of fights with the local people—a sad forecast of what was to happen in most of the places where Europeans and Native Americans would meet. But the Vikings did not make a permanent settlement in Vinland, and their American adventure was soon all but forgotten.

It would be another five hundred years before Europeans returned to the Americas and carved out a lasting foothold there. In the 1490s, Christopher Columbus's voyages across the Atlantic Ocean told Europeans that there was land on the other side of that ocean. Early in the sixteenth century Spain began colonizing Mexico, overthrowing the great empire of the Native American Aztec people and establishing Spanish rule. Soon Spanish adventurers were pushing northward to establish settlements in what is now New Mexico, in the southwestern United States.

Ships of other nations, meanwhile, busily probed North America's Atlantic coast. In the early seventeenth century two nations claimed parts of that coast. France took what is now Canada. Farther south, Great Britain established the string of coastal colonies that would one day become the United States. By the middle of the eighteenth century, Russians were beginning to cross from Asia to Alaska near where the prehistoric hunters had crossed. This time, however, the newcomers crossed the Bering Strait by sea instead of by land. On the northern Pacific coast of North America, far from their homeland, hunters and fur traders created a short-lived Russian culture.

Of all the European powers that set up colonies in North America, the British were most determined to populate the land.

The Spanish searched for gold and silver in the Southwest, and they eventually established some forts, trading posts, missions, settlements, and ranches there. But the great majority of Spanish colonists were in Mexico, not in the remote and rugged Southwest, which was called the Borderlands because it was far from the center of colonial life in Mexico City. In Canada, the French built a thriving business trading furs from the interior. Most of the settlers, however, were in a handful of cities and towns along the Saint Lawrence River. Fewer people were willing to leave France for the North American colony than the French government hoped. But the British colonies attracted large numbers of settlers, not just from the British Isles but from other parts of Europe as well.

At first there were only two British settlements: Jamestown, founded in Virginia in 1607, and Plymouth, founded in Massachusetts in 1620. Before many years had passed, the rest of the Atlantic coastline south of Canada was in British hands. Great Britain even took over small Dutch and Swedish colonies in New York and Delaware. Florida was never a British colony—the United States would acquire it from Spain in 1819. But by the 1730s everything between Canada and Florida was British and open to settlement.

And the settlers came. Some came for religious freedom, some hoped to win their fortunes in what they called the "New World," and some came simply to escape debt or the lack of opportunity in their homelands. Some worked as servants to pay for their passage across the Atlantic. Others came against their will, captured in Africa and brought to the colonies as enslaved laborers. By 1754, less than a century and a half after the founding of the Jamestown settlement, a million and a half people lived in the British colonies, compared with just 100,000 in French North America and fewer still in the Spanish Borderlands.

From the beginning, land beckoned the British colonists westward. Those who came early snapped up the good farmland and building sites along the coast. Soon people were moving inland, finding travel routes or learning about them from the local Native Americans, cutting trails and farm plots out of the dense forest. Newly arrived colonists looking for a place to call their own, children and grandchildren of early settlers who could not afford to buy property in the crowded towns their forebears had founded— these people pushed the edge of settlement westward a little at a time. By the 1750s the frontier had reached the summits of the Appalachian Mountains. The British tried to make those mountains into a barrier. They wanted to keep the colonists between the Appalachians and the Atlantic, where they could be counted, governed—and taxed. The colonists had other ideas, however, and by the time the Revolutionary War broke out in 1776 at least five thousand Americans had crossed the Appalachians to settle in the valley of the Ohio River. These pioneers experienced both the terror and the glory of the western frontier.

To Europeans the unexplored land on the western edge of the known world had always seemed to wear two faces. One face was lovely and inviting. Bartolomé de Las Casas, who came early to Mexico and wrote about Christopher Columbus's voyages, said that Columbus had declared, after gazing at the view from a mountain in Cuba, that "all that he had seen was so beautiful that

his eyes would never tire beholding so much beauty." Many saw America as fertile, fruitful, filled with timber and game—a vast land of endless, abundant bounty.

Yet the same land that could appear beautiful and generous could also seem dark and terrifying. William Bradford, leader of the 1620 Massachusetts colonists, called America "a hideous and desolate wilderness full of wild beasts and wild men." Colonists who fondly remembered the cities, villages, and tidy, well-farmed countryside of England found the untamed new land disturbing. Soon, though, they had begun to tame it. A colonist named Edward Johnson wrote in 1653 that what was once "a rocky, barren bushy, wild-woody wilderness" had become "a second England," thanks to the efforts of

When American artist Thomas Cole painted *Home in the Woods*, people were still carving homesteads out of the wilderness. The painting suggests an ideal vision of serene, self-sufficient frontier life. A closer view might have revealed some degree of discomfort or danger.

At first, settlers merely trickled west, but the wagon trains of the 1840s turned the trickle into a flood. Tragically, the flood wiped out many Native-American communities and even entire cultures.

people like him. Just as the first generation of colonists on the Atlantic coast struggled to create communities and ways of life similar to those they had known in England, the later settlers who pushed westward would work to rebuild the old, familiar world on a series of new frontiers.

The frontier of settlement kept moving, and the farther west it reached the faster it moved. It took more than a century and a half for the frontier to climb the Appalachians. Only a few decades after the Revolutionary War ended in 1783, the frontier had pushed all the way to the Mississippi River. By 1800 Americans were settling on the west bank of that river and were hungrily looking farther west toward territory that did not even belong to their country. Then, in 1803, the United States bought from France the region between the river and the Rocky Mountains. The next year the Lewis and Clark Expedition set out to survey that territory—and beyond it all the way to the Pacific Ocean. Other explorers soon crossed the Mississippi. So did fur trappers and traders. A few decades later wagon trains of settlers were inching across the central Plains, set aside by the U.S. Congress as Indian Territory, to claim land beyond the Rockies, on the Pacific coast. These pioneers called themselves emigrants, people who leave their country, because when they crossed the Rockies they were passing beyond the borders of the United States. The United States followed them, though, annexing territory in the Pacific Northwest, Texas, California, and the Southwest. By the time settlement began on the Great Plains in the 1870s, the entire West belonged to the United States.

"The oldest West was the Atlantic," wrote American historian Frederick Jackson Turner in 1908. "The West, at bottom, is a form of society rather than an area." When the first colonists staggered ashore at Jamestown—weary after the long voyage, half fearful of the dangerous New World, half expecting to find gold under every rock—the opening of the American West began. The adventure would continue for two centuries, and all kinds of people would have parts in it: men, women, and children of Native American, European, African, and Asian descent, governors and generals, chieftains and homemakers, builders and farmers and drifters. The story of the West is woven from all their stories, and it is told best in their own words.

A Series of Western Frontiers

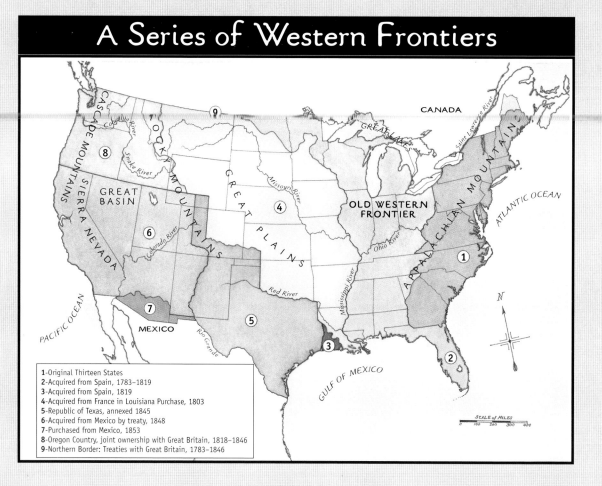

1-Original Thirteen States
2-Acquired from Spain, 1783–1819
3-Acquired from Spain, 1819
4-Acquired from France in Louisiana Purchase, 1803
5-Republic of Texas, annexed 1845
6-Acquired from Mexico by treaty, 1848
7-Purchased from Mexico, 1853
8-Oregon Country, joint ownership with Great Britain, 1818–1846
9-Northern Border: Treaties with Great Britain, 1783–1846

Chapter I

The Frontier

IN 1845, A NEW ENGLANDER named Josiah Bushnell Grinnell decided to settle on the western frontier. People told him that the West was to be found in Indiana, Illinois, or Wisconsin. "Then I passed along," he wrote in his book *Home of the Badgers*, "crossing great rivers and broad Prairies, and again I asked for the West. They said it was in Iowa." Grinnell went on a little farther and was told that he had not yet reached the West. People said, "But go, if you wish to see the West, days and days, hundreds and hundreds of miles up the Missouri—farther than from us to New England, and beyond the Rocky Mountains, and among the Snake Indians of Oregon, and you may find it."

As Grinnell discovered, "the West" was not a single place. America had many frontiers before the country reached its full size and was fully settled. For example, today the term *Northwest* refers to the Pacific Northwest states of Washington and Oregon. But two hundred years ago an American who spoke of "the Northwest" meant the Ohio River valley, which was then the nation's northwestern frontier. History books often call that early frontier the Old Northwest or the Northwest Territory.

As Americans moved west, they settled the Old Northwest first, then the area south of the Ohio River. When they crossed the Mississippi River, they leapfrogged across the Great Plains, the area between the river and the Rocky Mountains. For a time, Congress tried to set the plains aside for the Native Americans—including many who had been driven off their land east of the Mississippi by white settlement. Settlers passed through the Great Plains on their way to California, Oregon, and Utah.

When Americans began settling west of the Rockies and in Texas, those parts of North America did not even belong to the United States. Many Americans, however, felt that they *should*. People did not want Spanish or British territory to lie between the United States and the Pacific, creating a barrier to American settlement and possibly blocking trade. Some believed that the United States, with its new form of democratic government, had a special purpose—to occupy North America from "sea to shining sea," as the patriotic song "America, the Beautiful" would later say. By 1845, this idea was so widely accepted that newspaper editor John Louis O'Sullivan wrote in the *New York Post* that the clear fate, or "manifest destiny," of the American people was "to overspread the continent allotted by Providence for the free development of our yearly multiplying millions."

Driven by the vision that came to be called Manifest Destiny, the United States had already acquired more territory. By the end of the 1840s it had gained the Pacific Northwest from Britain as well as Texas, California, and the Southwest from Mexico. The country had marched all the way to the Pacific Ocean. Soon after, in the 1860s, Congress made the Great Plains available for settlement. Between the birth of the United States and the dawn of the twentieth century, Americans were busy opening one western frontier after another.

Defining the First Frontier: The Proclamation of 1763

France and Great Britain went to war in 1754. In the North American colonies, the conflict was known as the French and Indian War, and it ended in 1763 in a British victory. Great Britain won the Ohio River valley, which the French and British had fought to control. The Native Americans of the valley had also been fighting—to keep settlers off their lands. Hoping to end the Indian fighting and keep colonists from streaming to remote and ungovernable regions, the British government made a law called the Proclamation of 1763. In the name of King George III of Great Britain, it outlawed settlement beyond the summits of the Appalachian Mountains.

[W]HEREAS IT IS JUST and reasonable, and essential to our interest and the security of our colonies, that the several nations or tribes of Indians with whom we are connected, and who live under our protection, should not be molested or disturbed in the possession of such parts of our dominions and territories as, not having been ceded to or purchased by us, are reserved to them, or any of them, as their hunting-grounds; we do therefore, with the advice of our

Privy Council, declare it to be our royal will and pleasure, that no Governor or commander in chief, in any of our colonies . . . do presume for the present, and until our further pleasure is known, to grant warrants of survey or pass patents for any lands beyond the heads of sources of any of the rivers which fall into the Atlantic Ocean from the west or northwest; or upon any lands whatever, which, not having been ceded to or purchased by us, as aforesaid, are reserved to the said Indians, or any of them.

...And we do further strictly enjoin and require all persons whatever, who have either wilfully or inadvertently seated themselves upon any lands within the countries above described, or upon any other lands which, not having been ceded to or purchased by us, are still reserved to the said Indians as aforesaid, forthwith to remove themselves from such settlements.

—*Sanford Wexler,* Westward Expansion: An Eyewitness History.
New York: Facts On File, 1991, Appendix A.

THINK ABOUT THIS

1. How does the Proclamation of 1763 define the western limit of settlement?
2. Why do you think the king of England was concerned about protecting Indian lands?

The United States Moves into Indian Territory: The Treaty of Greenville

The Proclamation of 1763 failed to keep British colonists out of the Ohio River valley. After the colonies became the independent United States, the U.S. government started dividing the Ohio River

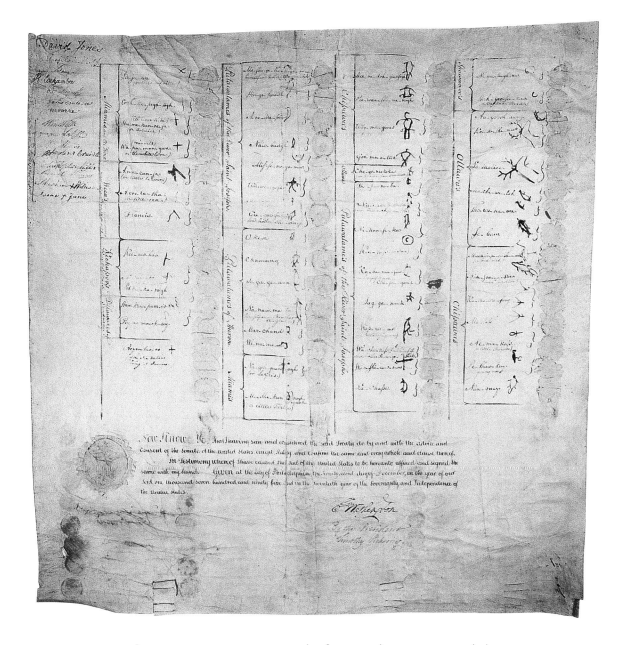

More than 1,100 Native-American chieftains and warriors signed the 1795 Treaty of Greenville, giving much of their land north of the Ohio River to the U.S. government. The Indians, who did not use written languages, drew symbols or creatures such as fish to represent their signatures.

valley into territories and townships for settlement. First, however, the government had to "buy" the land from the Native Americans. The purchases took the form of treaties. This passage is from the 1795 Treaty of Greenville, signed by General Anthony Wayne and nearly a hundred chiefs of the Wyandot, Delaware, Shawnee, Ottawa, Chippewa, Miami, Weea, Kickapoo, and Kaskaskia peoples. Under the treaty, the Indians gave up most of Ohio and part of Indiana. Other areas, such as Illinois and Michigan, were defined as Indian lands. But Americans would soon settle on those lands, leading to conflict.

TO PUT AN END to a destructive war, to settle all controversies, and to restore harmony and a friendly intercourse between the said United States, and Indian Tribes; Anthony Wayne, major-general, commanding the army of the United States, and sole commissioner for the good purposes abovementioned, and the said tribes of Indians, by their Sachems, chiefs, and warriors, met together at Greenville, the head quarters of the said army, have agreed on the following articles, which, when ratified by the President, with the advice and consent of the Senate of the United States, shall be binding on them and the said Indian tribes.

. . . If any citizen of the United States, or any other white person or persons, shall presume to settle upon the lands now relinquished by the United States, such citizen or other person shall be out of the protection of the United States; and the Indian tribe, on whose land the settlement shall be made, may drive off the settler, or punish him in such manner as they shall think fit; and because such settlements made without the consent of the United States, will be injurious to them as well as to the Indians, the United States shall be at liberty to break them up, and remove and punish the settlers as they shall think proper, and so effect the protection of the Indian lands herein before stipulated.

—*Sanford Wexler,* Westward Expansion: An Eyewitness History.
New York: Facts On File, 1991, Appendix A.

THINK ABOUT THIS

1. Why do you think British colonists ignored the Proclamation of 1763?
2. Under the Treaty of Greenville, what could the Indians do to a white person who settled on their land?
3. What could the United States government do to a white settler on Indian land?

Thomas Jefferson Looks toward the Pacific Ocean

When Thomas Jefferson became president of the United States in 1801, the Mississippi River was the western border of the country. Jefferson was curious about what lay beyond the river. He wanted to send explorers into the Louisiana Territory and beyond it to the Pacific Ocean. The first passage below is from a secret message Jefferson wrote to Congress, outlining his plan for an exploratory expedition. The message had to be secret because the Louisiana Territory belonged to France, which had just acquired it from Spain. The second passage was written six months later, after France had agreed to sell the Louisiana Territory to the United States. It is from a letter that Jefferson wrote to Meriwether Lewis, the man he chose to head the expedition.

AN INTELLIGENT OFFICER with ten or twelve chosen men, fit for the enterprize and willing to undertake it, taken from our posts, where they may be spared without inconvenience, might explore the whole line, even to the Western ocean, have conferences with the natives on the subject of commercial intercourse, get admission among them for our traders as others are admitted, agree on convenient deposits for an interchange of articles, and return with the information acquired in the course of two summers. *[Secret letter to Congress asking for funds for the exploration of the Louisiana Territory, December 1802]*

"An intelligent officer with ten or twelve chosen men, fit for the enterprize and willing to undertake it . . . might explore the whole line, even to the Western ocean."

THE OBJECT OF YOUR MISSION is to explore the Missouri River, & such principal stream of it, as, by it's course and communication with the waters of the Pacific ocean, whether the Columbia, Oregon, Colorado or any other river may offer the most direct & practicable water communication across the continent for the purposes of commerce. *[Letter of instruction to Meriwether Lewis of the Lewis and Clark expedition, June 1803]*

—*Julian Boyd, editor,* The Papers of Thomas Jefferson. *Princeton, NJ: Princeton University Press, 1950.*

THINK ABOUT THIS

1. What do you think was Jefferson's main reason for exploring the West?

2. Does the letter to Lewis contain a specific instruction not found in the message to Congress?

A Senator's 1827 Call for American Expansion

Thomas Hart Benton was a senator from Missouri. His thirty-year political career began in 1821, and he became famous as a supporter of the West. Benton believed in Manifest Destiny even before the term existed, as shown in this newspaper editorial, which appeared in the *St. Louis Beacon* in 1827. Benton is criticizing the Adams-Onís Treaty of 1819, which gave Florida to the United States and Texas to Spain. The "valley of the Mississippi" that he mentions means all of the territory drained by rivers that flow into the Mississippi, including the Red River and other streams in northern Texas.

THE WESTERN PEOPLE have a claim from the laws of God and nature to the exclusive possession of the entire valley of the Mississippi. This magnificent valley was, and it ought to be, theirs, in all its extent and circumference—to the head spring of every stream that drains it, to the summit ridge of the mountains which enclose it. It was, and ought to be, theirs, in all its borders and dimensions, with all its woods and groves, with all its fountains, springs, and floods. Not an inch of its soil should be trod, not a drop of its waters should be drunk, by any foreign power. The American people alone should have it.

—*Eugene C. Barker,* Mexico and Texas, 1821–1835.
New York: Russell & Russell, 1928.

THINK ABOUT THIS

1. Who were the "American people," in Benton's opinion?
2. What do you think Benton meant by the "laws of God and nature"?

Americans and the Frontier: A Historian's View

In 1893, a young Wisconsin professor named Frederick Jackson Turner went to Chicago for a meeting of the American Historical Society. There he presented a paper called "The Significance of the Frontier in American History." Turner's paper shaped the thinking of several generations of historians. In it, he said that the settlement of the frontier was the key event of American history. It had forged the American character. Shortly before Turner presented his paper, the superintendent of the U.S. Census had declared that the frontier—the boundary between settled and unsettled land— had disappeared in 1880. A "great historic movement" had ended, Turner said, and now it was the historian's task to discover what it had meant.

UP TO OUR OWN DAY American history has been in large degree the history of the colonization of the Great West. . . . American social development has been continually beginning over again on the frontier. This perennial rebirth, this fluidity of American life, this expansion westward with its new opportunities, its continuous touch with the simplicity of primitive society, furnish the forces dominating American character. The true point of view in the history of this nation is not the Atlantic coast, it is the Great West. . . . In this advance, the frontier is the outer edge of the wave—the meeting point between savagery and civilization. . . . From the time the mountains rose between the pioneer and the seaboard, a new order of Americanism arose. The West and the East began to get out of touch with each other. The settlements from the sea to the mountains kept connection with the rear and had a certain solidarity. But

The west is dead my Friend.
But writers hold the seed
And what they sow
Will live and grow
Again to those who Read

C. M. Russell
1917

By 1917, little more than a century after the Lewis and Clark expedition, American artist Charles M. Russell could write "the west is dead." But although the frontier had vanished, artists and writers kept its legends and its legacy alive.

the over-mountain men grew more and more independent. . . . From the conditions of frontier life came intellectual traits of profound importance. The works of travelers along each frontier from colonial days onward describe certain common traits, and these traits have, while softening down, still persisted. . . . The result is that to the frontier the American intellect owes its striking characteristics. That coarseness and strength combined with acuteness and inquisitiveness; that practical, inventive turn of mind, quick to find expedients; that masterful grasp of material things, lacking in the artistic but powerful to effect great ends; that restless, nervous energy; that dominant individualism, working for good and for evil, and withal that buoyancy and exuberance which comes with freedom—these are the traits of the frontier, or traits called out elsewhere because of the existence of the frontier.

—*Frederick Jackson Turner,* The Frontier in American History. *New York: Holt, Rinehart, and Winston, 1920.*

THINK ABOUT THIS

1. What traits did Turner see as typical of Americans?
2. Do you think Turner was correct? If so, why?

A Party of Explorers (1851) captures the sense of awe and mystery that many people reported feeling when they entered the wild, unknown landscapes of the West.

Chapter 2

The Explorers

THE AMERICAN FRONTIER did not move westward on its own, like a rising tide. It was pushed westward by bold individuals who ventured into the great unknown and returned to tell others what they had found. These explorers opened the way. Using the routes they pioneered and the information they gathered, hunters, traders, missionaries, and settlers followed them west.

The exploration of North America took place by sea and on land. The seagoing exploration of the coasts began with Christopher Columbus in the 1490s and continued for several centuries. Long before anyone went far inland, ship captains had observed and mapped most of the Atlantic coastline. During the sixteenth century, after European mariners had discovered a route around the southern tip of South America, ships began to reach the Pacific coast of North America. Sir Francis Drake of England, who landed somewhere near San Francisco Bay in the 1570s, was just one of those who explored parts of the west coast before any settlements had taken root on the east coast.

Seafarers and geographers slowly pieced together the map of the

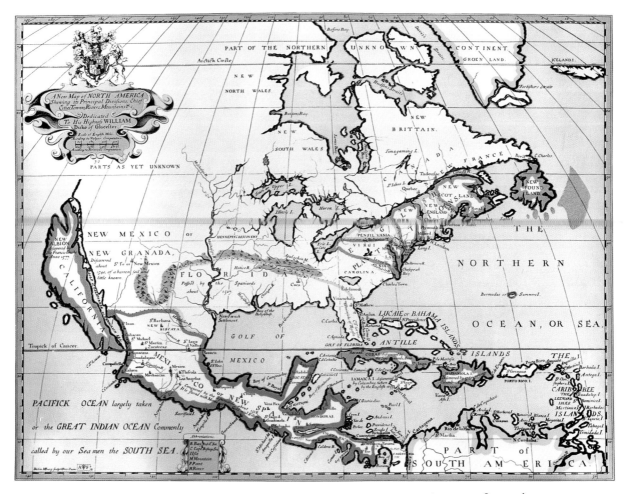

Old maps, such as this early-eighteenth-century British map of North America, are primary sources that tell historians how people in various eras viewed their world. This map, for example, repeats an old geographic mistake by showing California as an island. The northern and northwestern parts of the continent are "as yet unknown."

American coastlines. By the late eighteenth century, North America's outline was fairly well known, except for its Arctic and Alaskan coasts. Its interior, however, was still a mystery. Maps showed the settled lands along the Atlantic coast, the Appalachian Mountains, the Great Lakes, and a few sketchy lines to hint at the Ohio and Mississippi Rivers, but the heart of the continent was a big blank space.

A few early European travelers had made wide-ranging journeys through that blank space. Some were Spanish conquistadors, military conquerors who were also explorers. Hernán de Soto had cut a bloody path through the Southeast in the early 1540s, looking in vain for gold. Around the same time, Francisco Vásquez de Coronado led an expedition through the Southwest and into the plains, also looking for riches. He did not find any, although some of his men stumbled upon a great natural treasure, the Grand Canyon of the Colorado River.

Early travels produced some geographic knowledge, but the real exploration of inland North America did not begin until settlements were established up and down the Atlantic coast. The settlements were jumping-off points for restless folk who kept stretching the frontier as they searched for new hunting grounds or places to settle. Later, after the frontier crossed the Mississippi River, the U.S. government sent official explorers out to survey and map the West.

Even after the government took over the task of exploration, the spirit of individual adventure remained alive. In 1869 John Wesley Powell completed what some historians call the last great exploratory expedition in the United States outside Alaska—the first boat journey down the Colorado River, through the same Grand Canyon that Coronado's men had viewed with amazement more than three hundred years earlier. Powell received a little help from the government, but he paid for the trip largely out of his own pocket, simply because he wanted to discover what the river was like. The desire to know what lay beyond the next mountain or around the next river bend had lured explorers into the American West since colonial times.

Daniel Boone in Kentucky

Daniel Boone was a frontiersman who became a symbol of the American pioneer after his adventures were described in a 1784 book by John Filson, who claimed to be writing Boone's own words, although not all historians accept that claim. Boone led the first group of settlers from the British colonies across the Appalachians into Kentucky in 1775, just before the outbreak of the Revolutionary War. Here Filson describes, supposedly in Boone's words, an earlier scouting trip into Kentucky.

IT WAS THE FIRST OF MAY, in the year 1769, that I resigned my domestic happiness for a time, and left my family and peacable habitation on the Yadkin River, in North-Carolina, to wander through the wilderness of America, in quest of the country of Kentucke, in company with John Finley, John Stewart, Joseph Holden, James Monay, and William Cool. We proceeded successfully, and after a long and fatiguing journey through a mountainous wilderness, in a westward direction, on the seventh day of June following we found ourselves on the Red-River, where John Finley had formerly been trading with the Indians, and, from the top of an eminence, saw with pleasure the beautiful level of Kentucke. . . . We found everywhere abundance of wild beasts of all sorts, through this vast forest. The buffaloes were more frequent than I have seen cattle in the settlements, browzing on the leaves of the cane, or croping the herbage on those extensive plains, fearless, because ignorant, of the violence of man. Sometimes we saw hundreds in a drove, and the numbers about the salt springs were amazing. In this forest, the habitation of beasts of every kind natural to America, we practiced hunting with great success until the twenty-second day of December following.

"We found everywhere abundance of wild beasts of all sorts."

[Boone later separated from his companions, but his brother, Squire Boone, joined him.]

. . .We continued not in a state of indolence, but hunted every day, and prepared a little cottage to defend us from the winter storms. We remained there undisturbed during the Winter; and on the first day of May, 1770, my brother returned home to the settlement by himself, for a new recruit of horses and ammunition, leaving me by myself, without bread, salt or sugar, without company of my fellow creatures, or even a horse or dog. I confess I never before was under greater necessity of exercising philosophy and fortitude. A few days I passed uncomfortably. The idea of a beloved wife and family, and their anxiety on account of my absence and exposed situation, made sensible impressions on my heart. A thousand dreadful apprehensions presented themselves to my view, and had undoubtedly disposed me to melancholy, if further indulged.

—*John Filson,* The Discovery, Settlement and Present State of Kentucke.
New York: Corinth Books, 1962. Originally published in 1784.

Think about This

1. How did the buffalo of Kentucky compare with the cattle of the settlements?
2. When Boone found himself alone in the wilderness, what was his greatest hardship?

Lewis and Clark Cross the Continent

Meriwether Lewis and William Clark led the expedition that President Thomas Jefferson sent west in 1804 from Saint Louis to explore the lands beyond the Mississippi. The expedition reached the Pacific Ocean in what is now Oregon and, in 1806, returned to Saint Louis. Both leaders kept journals on the trip. In these books they recorded details of expedition business and descriptions of geography, wildlife, and Native Americans. They also recorded some private thoughts and experiences along the way.

FROM MERIWETHER LEWIS'S JOURNAL:
SUNDAY AUGUST 18TH 1805

rout *route*

This morning while Capt Clark was busily engaged in preparing for his rout, I exposed some articles to barter with the Indians for horses as I wished a few at this moment to relieve the men who were going with Capt Clark from the labour of carrying their baggage, and also one to keep here in order to pack the meat to camp which the hunters might kill. I soon obtained three very good horses. for which I gave an uniform coat, a pair of leggings, a few handkerchiefs, three knives and some other small articles the whole of which did not cost more than about 20$ in the U'States. the Indians seemed quite as well pleased with their bargin as i was. . . . This day I completed my thirty first year, and conceived that I had in all human probability now existed about half the period which I am to remain in this Sublunary world. I reflected that I had as yet done but little, very little, indeed, to further the happiness of the human race, or to advance the information of the succeeding generation. I viewed with regret the many hours I have spent in indolence, and now soarly feel the way of that information which those hours would have given me had they been judiciously expended. but since they are past and cannot be recalled, I dash from me the gloomy

Meriwether Lewis was painted by American artist Rembrandt Peale, who also produced well-known portraits of Thomas Jefferson and George Washington.

Like Lewis, William Clark had his portrait painted by Peale. The two images are primary sources for information about the explorers' appearances.

thought, and resolved in future, to redouble my exertions and at least endeavour to promote those two primary objects of human existence, by giving them the aid of that portion of talents which nature and fortune have bestoed on me; or in future, to live *for mankind,* as I have heretofore lived *for myself.*

FROM WILLIAM CLARK'S JOURNAL:

TUESDAY AUGUST 3RD 1806

last night the Musquetors was so troublesom that no one of the party Slept half the night. for my part I did not sleep one hour. those tormenting insects found their way into My beare and tormented me the whole night. they are not less noumerous or troublesom this morning. at 2 miles passed the enterance of Jo. Field's Creek 35 yds wide imediately above a high bluff which is falling into the river very fast. on the side of this bluff I saw some of the Mountain Bighorn animals. I assended the hill below the Bluff. the Musquetors were so noumerous that I could not Shute with any certainty and therefore soon returned to the Canoes.

beare *netting meant to keep insects out of a camp bed*

—*Reuben Gold Thwaites, editor,* Original Journals of the Lewis and Clark Expedition, 1804–1806. *New York: Dodd, Mead, and Company, 1905.*

THINK ABOUT THIS

1. What were Lewis's two most important goals in life?

2. How would you compare the two men's concerns in these entries?

Zebulon Pike: A Spy in Spanish Territory

Zebulon Montgomery Pike was a U.S. Army officer. In 1806 his commander sent him to survey the upper Red and Rio Grande Rivers, near the border of Spanish territory. The United States and Spain disagreed about that border, and many historians think that Pike was more of a spy than an explorer—his commander may have wanted to make Spain angry enough to start a war between the two nations, although Pike probably knew nothing of such a plan. Pike and his men trespassed on Spanish territory, and a Spanish patrol caught them and took them to the city of Santa Fe before returning them to U.S. territory. Pike's descriptions and maps gave Americans their first glimpse of the Spanish capital in what is now New Mexico.

"You come to reconnoitre our country, do you?"

ITS APPEARANCE FROM a distance, struck my mind with the same effect as a fleet of flat-bottomed boats, which are seen in the spring and fall seasons, descending the Ohio river. There are two churches, the magnificence of whose steeples form a striking contrast to the miserable appearance of the houses. On the north side of the town is the square of soldiers houses, equal to 120 or 140 [houses] on each flank. The public square is in the centre of the town; on the north side of which is situated the palace (as they term it) or government house, with the quarters for guards, &c [etc.]. The other side of the square is occupied by the clergy and public officers. In general the houses have a shed before the front, some of which have a flooring of brick; the consequence is, that the streets are very narrow, say in general 25 feet. The supposed population is 4,500 souls. On our entering the town, the crowd was great, and followed us to the government house.

When we dismounted, we were ushered in through various rooms, the floors of which were covered with skins of buffalo, or some other animal. We waited in a chamber for some time, until his excellency appeared, when we rose, and the following conversation took place in French.

Governor. Do you speak French?

Pike. Yes, sir.

Governor. You come to reconnoitre our country, do you?

Pike. I marched to reconnoitre our own.

Governor. In what character are you?

Pike. In my proper character, an officer of the United States army.

—*Donald Jackson, editor,* The Journals of Zebulon Montgomery Pike. *Norman, OK: University of Oklahoma Press, 1966.*

THINK ABOUT THIS

1. How would you describe Pike's attitude toward the Spanish leader who questioned him?
2. Does Pike's report contain any information that might be useful to a military force invading Santa Fe? If so, what?
3. What difference did Pike notice between the churches and the houses of Santa Fe?

The Pathfinder: John Charles Frémont in Oregon

John Charles Frémont was a soldier who later became a politician and ran unsuccessfully for president in 1856. Earlier he had become known as "The Pathfinder" after leading several government-sponsored exploring and mapmaking missions in the Rocky Mountains and the West. On an 1843 journey that carried him from the

Army officer and explorer John Charles Frémont was the son-in-law of Thomas Hart Benton, the senator who supported American claims to the West. Benton pulled strings to put Frémont in charge of a series of exploring expeditions that advanced those claims.

banks of the Columbia River to Pyramid Lake in Nevada, he passed through what is now the Fremont National Forest in south-central Oregon. This passage is reprinted from his 1851 report to the government, which covers his explorations from 1842 through 1844 and is based on his journals.

DECEMBER 16.—We travelled this morning through snow about three feet deep, which, being crusted, very much cut the feet of our animals. The mountain still gradually rose; we crossed several spring heads covered with quaking asp; otherwise it was all pine forest. The air was dark with falling snow, which every where weighed down the trees. The depths of the forest were profoundly still; and below, we scarce felt a breath of the wind which whirled the snow through their branches. . . .

Towards noon the forest looked clear ahead, appearing suddenly to terminate, and beyond a certain point we could see no trees. Riding rapidly ahead to this spot, we found ourselves on the verge of a vertical and rocky wall of the mountain. At our feet—more than a thousand feet below—we looked into a green prairie country, in which a beautiful lake, some twenty miles in length, was spread along the foot of the mountains, its shores bordered with green grass. Just then the sun broke out among the clouds, and illuminated the country below, while around us the storm raged fiercely. Not a particle of ice was to be seen on the lake, or snow on its borders, and all was like summer or spring. The glow of the sun in the valley below brightened up our hearts with sudden pleasure; and we made the woods ring with joyful shouts to those behind; and gradually, as each came up, he stopped to enjoy the unexpected scene. Shivering on snow three feet deep, and stiffening in cold north winds, we exclaimed at once that the names of Summer Lake and Winter Ridge should be applied to these two proximate places of such sudden and violent contrast.

> *"The glow of the sun in the valley below brightened up our hearts with sudden pleasure; and we made the woods ring with joyful shouts to those behind."*

—*John L. Stewart,* Fremont's Greatest Western Exploration, Volume 1: The Dalles to Pyramid Lake: In Fremont's own words, with modern maps. *Vancouver, WA: SET, 1999.*

John Wesley Powell Maps the Grand Canyon

John Wesley Powell was a schoolteacher who fought for the Union in the Civil War. Drawn to exploration in the West, in 1869 he took nine men and four boats on a thrilling and perilous 1,500-mile ride down the Green and Colorado Rivers through Wyoming, Utah, and Arizona. It was the first known boat journey through the Grand Canyon, and it made Powell an authority on the geography of the Colorado Plateau, one of the last parts of North America to be explored. The following passages are from his diary of the voyage. They were written when the explorers had been on the rivers for about ten weeks and were ready to enter the Grand Canyon, which Powell calls "the Great Unknown."

By the time John Wesley Powell posed for this portrait, the camera had become a valuable tool for producing primary sources. It recorded the final stages of the opening of the West.

AUGUST 13.

We are now ready to start on our way down the Great Unknown. Our boats, tied to a common stake, are chafing each other, as they are tossed by the fretful river. They ride high and buoyant, for their loads are lighter than we could desire. We have but a month's rations remaining. The flour has been resifted through the mosquito-net sieve; the spoiled bacon has been dried, and the worst of it boiled; the few pounds of dried apples have been spread in the sun, and reshrunken to their normal bulk; the sugar has all melted, and gone on its way down the river; but we have a large sack of coffee. The lighting of the boats has this advantage: they will ride the waves better, and we shall have but little to carry when we make a portage.

We are three-quarters of a mile in the depths of the earth, and the great river shrinks into insignificance, as it dashes its angry waves against the walls and cliffs, that rise to the world above; they are but puny ripples, and we but pigmies, running up and down the sands, or lost among the boulders.

We have an unknown distance yet to run; an unknown river yet to explore. What falls there are, we know not; what rocks beset the channel, we know not; what walls rise over the river, we know not. The men talk as cheerfully as ever; jests are bandied about freely this morning; but to me the cheer is somber and the jests are ghastly. . . .

AUGUST 14.

At daybreak we walk down the bank of the river, on a little sandy beach, to take a view of a new feature in the canyon. Heretofore, hard rocks have given us bad river; soft rocks, smooth water; and a series of rocks harder than any we have experienced sets in. The river enters the granite!

We can see but a little way into the gorge, but it looks threatening. . . .

About eleven o'clock we hear a great roar ahead, and approach it very cautiously. The sound grows louder and louder as we run, and at last we find ourselves above a long, broken fall, with edges and pinnacles of rock obstructing the river. There is a descent of, perhaps, seventy-five or eighty feet in a third of a mile, and the rushing waters break into great waves on the rocks, and lash themselves into a mad, white foam. We can land just above, but there is no foothold on either side by which we can make a portage. It is nearly a thousand feet to the top of the granite, so it will be impossible to carry our boats around . . . we must run the rapid, or abandon the river. There is no hesitation.

> *"We must run the rapid, or abandon the river. There is no hesitation."*

—*John Wesley Powell,* Down the Colorado: Diary of the First Trip through the Grand Canyon, 1869. *New York: E.P. Dutton, 1969. Originally published in 1875.*

THINK ABOUT THIS

1. Can you imagine what it must have been like to ride the waves of the Colorado deep within the earth?
2. How did Powell feel as he looked up the canyon walls?
3. What were the advantages of the boats being light? At this time in the journey, were there any disadvantages?
4. How dangerous was this trip?

Chapter 3

Mountain Men and Miners

FUR, NOT FARMLAND, drew some of the first adventurers westward. One of North America's most valuable resources was the fur pelt, or skin, of the water-dwelling beaver. Beaver fur, when removed from the skin and pressed into a thick, felt-like cloth, is smooth, sleek, and waterproof. Hats and capes made of it were prized in Europe—so much so that by 1600 or so the beaver population was nearly wiped out in most of Europe. Imported pelts from Russia filled the gap until Europeans discovered that the waterways of North America teemed with beaver.

Colonists in Canada and along the Atlantic coast trapped beaver or traded with the Indians for pelts. So many millions of pelts were shipped to England and France that by the 1770s beaver were almost extinct in eastern North America. Trappers and traders kept moving west to find fresh sources of pelts in unexplored streams and lakes. When explorers such as Lewis and Clark and Zebulon Pike returned from beyond the Mississippi and told of the abundant wildlife of the West, the fur hunters quickly crossed the river.

George Caleb Bingham's *Fur Traders Descending the Mississippi* (1845) commemorates the rugged adventurers who went west for profit but made major contributions to geographic knowledge. Bingham grew up in Missouri and as a young man traveled along the Missouri and Mississippi Rivers, capturing scenes along these water highways of the West.

Jim Bridger was one of the best-known Mountain Men. Among other achievements, he was the first white explorer to describe Utah's Great Salt Lake. Its saltiness convinced Bridger that he had reached the Pacific Ocean.

Among the first fur trappers into the West were Manuel Lisa, a Spanish citizen of New Orleans, and his partner George Drouillard, who had traveled with Lewis and Clark. Between 1807 and 1811 they explored the Missouri and Yellowstone Rivers in the northern Great Plains. At the same time, a fur trader named John Jacob Astor established an outpost near the mouth of the Columbia River in the Pacific Northwest, where Lewis and Clark had built their winter camp.

Conflicts with the Native Americans, as well as the War of 1812, between Great Britain and the United States, halted the western fur trade for a time. In the 1820s the trade picked up again, and a new generation of frontiersmen, called the Mountain Men, probed the Rocky Mountains in search of furs. Their purpose was business, but the Mountain Men were also explorers who knew more about the rivers, mountain passes, weather, wildlife, and people of the American West than anyone else of their day. Among them were Jim Bridger, who discovered a pass through the Rockies that many later travelers used, and Christopher "Kit" Carson, who accompanied Frémont on several of his expeditions.

Fur was not the only resource to draw people westward. Ever since Columbus, European explorers in North America had looked for gold, hoping to find rich civilizations like those the Spanish had conquered in Mexico and Peru. Although no such civilizations existed in North America, golden treasure lay waiting to be uncovered in California.

Americans began settling in California in the 1820s, even though California was officially part of Mexico. In 1846 the United States declared war on Mexico, and about two years later Mexico signed a peace treaty that turned over 1.2 million square miles of its territory—everything west of Texas and the Rockies and south of Oregon—to the United States. During the same year a mill worker near Sacramento, California, found gold in a stream. News leaked out, and by the following summer the gold rush of 1849 was under way. Thousands of prospectors called Forty-Niners made their way to California's Sierra Nevada, each expecting to claim a fortune in gold nuggets and dust. Very few of them ever made their fortunes, but many remained in California, along with the merchants, cooks, entertainers, and others who had supplied the mining camps. The same thing happened during the 1860s after gold strikes in Nevada, Colorado, Idaho, and Montana. The lure of instant wealth led to the birth of new communities across the West.

Jedediah Smith in Northern California

Some historians call Jedediah Smith the greatest Mountain Man of them all. Born in New York State in 1799, he joined a Saint Louis fur-trading company in 1822. A few years later he led the first American expedition across the Great Basin, the desert region between the Rocky Mountains and California. Although Smith's diaries were lost, a family friend had copied some of them, including this passage. It tells of an exciting encounter on a beaver-hunting trip through northern California in 1828, three years before Smith died in an Indian attack near the Arkansas River.

7TH APRIL. W N W 8 MILES. At 2 miles from camp crossed a creek 30 yards wide rapid and stoney Bottom running SW and having some Beaver sign. 3 Miles farther struck a creek same size and running SW but so deep that I was obliged to follow it up 3 Miles to find a ford at which place I encamped. . . . In the evening we shot several Bear and they ran into thickets that were convenient. Several of us followed one that was Badly wounded into a thicket. We went on foot because the thicket was too close to admit a Man on horse back.

> *"At that moment the Bear sprang towards us with open mouth and making no pleasant noise."*

As we advanced I saw one and shot him in the head when he immediately fell—Apparently dead. I went in to bring him out without loading my gun and when I arrived within 4 yards of the place where the Bear lay the man that was following me close behind spoke and said "He is alive". I told him in answer that he was certainly dead and was observing the one I had shot so intently that I did not see one which lay close by his side which was the one that the man behind me had reference to. At that moment the Bear sprang towards us with open mouth and making no pleasant noise.

Fortunately the thicket was close on the bank of the creek and the second [I saw him] spring I plunged headfirst into the water. The Bear ran over the man next to me and made a furious rush at the third man Joseph Lapointe. But Lapointe had by good fortune a Bayonet fixed on his gun and as the Bear came in he gave him a severe wound which caused him to change his course and run into another thicket close at hand. We followed him there and found another in company with him. One of them we killed and the other went off Badly wounded.

—*Maurice Sullivan, editor,* The Travels of Jedediah Smith: A Documentary Outline, Including the Journal of the Great American Pathfinder. *Santa Ana, CA: Fine Arts Press, 1934.*

"Whatever He Might Be": James Beckwourth's First Buffalo

James P. Beckwourth was a Mountain Man of part African-American descent. Like Smith, during the 1820s he worked for William Henry Ashley, who ran a fur-trading company in Saint Louis. Beckwourth called Ashley "the general" because he was an officer of the Missouri Territory's militia, the force of armed citizens assigned to defend the territory in an emergency. Beckwourth later lived among the Crow Indians and then settled in California, where he told his life story to a man named Thomas Bonner. When Bonner published it in 1856, some of Beckwourth's old-time comrades claimed that it contained a few exaggerations and outright lies. This account of a hunting trip along the Platte River, however, is probably true.

ENCOURAGED WITH MY SUCCESS, I climbed a tree to get a fairer view of the ground. Looking around from my elevated position, I perceived some large, dark-colored animal grazing on the side of a hill, some mile and a half distant. I was determined to have a shot at him, whatever he might be. I knew meat was in demand, and that fellow, well stored, was worth more than a thousand teal ducks.

I therefore approached, with the greatest precaution, to within fair rifle-shot distance, scrutinizing him very closely, and still unable to make out what he was. I could see no horns; and if he was a bear, I thought him an enormous one. I took sight of him over my faithful rifle, which had never failed me, and then set it down, to contemplate the huge animal still farther. Finally, I resolved to let fly; taking good aim, I pulled [the] trigger, the rifle cracked, and I then made rapid retreat toward the camp. After running about two hundred yards, and hearing nothing in movement behind me, I ventured to look round, and, to my great joy, I saw the animal had fallen.

Continuing my course on to the camp, I encountered the general, who, perceiving the blood on my hands, addressed me, "Have you shot anything, Jim?"

I replied, "Yes, sir."

"What have you shot?"

"Two deer and something else," I answered.

"And what is the something else?" he inquired.

"I do not know, sir."

"What did he look like?" the general interrogated. "Had he horns?"

"I saw no horns, sir."

"What color was the animal?"

"You can see him, general," I replied, "by climbing yonder tree."

The general ascended the tree accordingly, and looking through

BECKWOURTH.

session of the surrounding country. Beckwourth, in spite of the sad example he witnessed of aboriginal barbarity, soon became friendly with the red men, and, as genial companions, they accompanied him on his hunting excursions.

The great field of profitable enterprise at this early day was adventures in fur companies. St. Louis was the head-quarters of the hunters and trappers; they were the men of mark, and naturally inspired ambitious spirits with the desire to join in their pursuits. Beckwourth very naturally found a place among them, and, in the immediate employment of General Ashley, a name familiar to the people of the entire Union, he started with some brave mountaineers for the great Western wilderness. Disaster attended his first expedition. To such an extremity was he brought, that he would have died from suffering and starvation but for the most providential appearance of some friendly Indians. Arriving at last safely at his father's house, he says his feelings were akin to the sailor's just returned from sea. He rose in his own estimation, however, from having made a trip to the wild West, and even while reflecting upon what he had endured, and resolving in his own mind to stay at home, General Ashley prevailed upon him to take "another trip." Promptly starting on his perilous journey, he indulges in rhapsody upon the beauties of spring; and says that unfolding nature presented so many charms, that his previous sufferings were soon obliterated from his mind. He saw nothing but the trees clothing themselves in their richest verdure, flowers unvailing their beauties on every side, and heard nothing but birds from every bough caroling their sweetest songs.

On arriving at his place of destination he found his companions, thirty-four in number, reduced in health, in weakly condition, and in a discouraged state of mind. The promised supplies had not arrived, and it was in vain that General Ashley endeavored to infuse fresh courage into the breasts of starving men. There were no jokes, no fireside stories, no fun; each

Beckwourth was on familiar terms. Taking advantage of his journeying to call on his little playmates, to his horror he discovered the whole of them—eight in number, from one to fourteen years of age—lying in various positions in the door-yard, with their bodies mangled, their scalps torn off, and the warm life-blood still oozing from the gaping wounds. In the door-way lay their father, and near him their mother—they all had shared the same fate.

At ten years of age Beckwourth was bound out to a mechanical trade, but, as might be supposed from his subsequent life, he could not long endure discipline, and consequently, growing into a stout boy, he quarreled with his master. The result was that young Beckwourth received from his father a handsome sum of money, a good horse, many wholesome precepts and a paternal blessing, and then started upon what was destined to be a most eventful life.

His first employment after he became his own master was as "hunter" to a party headed by Colonel R. M. Johnson, afterward Vice-President of the United States, bound for the "lead mines," now so familiar as Galena, Illinois. At this place a treaty was made with the Sacs and Foxes, Indian tribes then in pos-

A page from an article in an old issue of *Harper's* magazine on the adventurous life of James Beckwourth.

his spy-glass, which he always carried, he exclaimed, "A buffalo, by heavens!" and, coming nimbly down the tree, he gave orders for us to take a couple of horses, and go and dress the buffalo, and bring him back to camp.

I suggested that two horses could not carry the load; six were therefore dispatched, and they all came back well packed with his remains. There was great rejoicing throughout the camp at such bountiful provision, and all fears of starvation were removed, at least for the present.

—*The Life and Adventures of James P. Beckwourth, Mountaineer, Scout, and Pioneer,* written from his own dictation by Thomas D. Bonner. New York: Harper & Brothers, 1856.

THINK ABOUT THIS

1. Why do you think Beckwourth did not recognize the buffalo?

2. What character trait most describes Beckwourth?

A Fur Trader Describes the Rocky Mountains

Joshua Pilcher was born in 1790 in Virginia. When he was a boy his family took the Wilderness Road, pioneered by Daniel Boone, to Kentucky. Pilcher later moved to Saint Louis and, in 1819, joined the Missouri Fur Company. As a fur trader he journeyed through Oregon Country and western Canada. In the 1830s he went to work for the U.S. government's Indian service. He eventually became superintendent of Indian Affairs at Saint Louis. This passage comes from a letter that Pilcher wrote to U.S. Secretary of War John H. Eaton in 1829.

THE ROCKY MOUNTAINS are deemed by many to be impassable, and to present the barrier which will arrest the westward march of the American population. The man must know but little of the American people who supposes that they can be stopped by any thing in the shape of mountains, deserts, seas, or rivers; and he can know nothing at all of the mountains in question, to suppose that they are impassable. I have been familiar with these mountains for three years, and have crossed them often, and at various points between the latitude 42 and 54; that is to say, between the head waters of the Rio Colorado of the gulf of California, and the Athabasca of the polar sea. I have, therefore, the means to know something about them, and a right to oppose my knowledge to the suppositions of strangers. I say, then, that nothing is more easily passed than these mountains. Wagons and carriages may cross them in a state of nature without difficulty, and with little delay in the day's journey.

Athabasca of the polar sea *Canada's Athabasca River, which flows northward and empties into Lake Athabasca, not into the Arctic Ocean as Pilcher thought*

—*Archer Butler Hulbert, editor,* Where Rolls Oregon: Prophet and Pessimist Look Northwest. *Denver, CO: Stewart Commission of Colorado College and Denver Public Library, 1933.*

THINK ABOUT THIS

1. Why did Pilcher think that Americans could settle beyond the Rocky Mountains?
2. How would Pilcher have described the American attitude toward a challenge?

A Woman's View of Gold-Rush Life

After the eager Forty-Niners rushed to the Sierra Nevada gold-fields, others followed to provide goods and services to the miners. In the spring of 1851 a physician named Fayette Clappe left San Francisco for the Feather River in northern California. Accompanying him was his wife, Louise Amelia Clappe, who described their year in the "diggings" in a series of letters to her sister on the East Coast. She signed the letters with the pen name "Dame Shirley," expecting them to be published. The letters give a vivid picture of the often difficult and dangerous life of the gold rush camps. Here she describes events that took place a few months before she arrived.

THOSE WHO WORKED in the mines during the fall of 1850 were extremely fortunate; but, alas! The Monte fiend ruined hundreds! Shall I tell you the fate of two of the most successful of these gold hunters? From poor men, they found themselves at the end of a few weeks, absolutely rich. Elated with their good fortune, seized with a mania for Monte, in less than a year, these unfortunates—so lately respectable and intelligent—became a pair of drunken gamblers. One of them at this present writing, works for five dollars a day and boards himself out of that; the other actually suffers for the necessaries of life—a too common result of scenes in the mines.

Monte
a gambling game

boards himself
pays for his food and lodging

There were but few that dared to remain in the mountains during the winter for fear of being buried in the snow; of which at that time they had a most vague idea. . . . Contrary to the general expectation, the weather was delightful until about the middle of March; it then commenced storming, and continued to snow and rain incessantly for three weeks. Supposing that the rainy season had passed, hundreds had arrived on the river during the previous month. The snow, which fell several feet in depth on the mountains, rendered the trail impassable and entirely stopped the pack trains; provisions soon became scarce, and the sufferings of these unhappy men were, indeed, extreme. Some adventurous spirits, with true Yankee hardihood, forced their way through the snow to the Frenchman's ranch, and packed flour on their backs, for more than forty miles! The first meal that arrived sold for three dollars a pound. Many subsisted for days on nothing but barley, which is kept here to feed the pack mules on. One unhappy individual who could not obtain even a little barley, for love or money, and had eaten nothing for three days, forced his way out to the Spanish rancho fourteen miles distant, and in less than an hour after his arrival, had devoured twenty-seven biscuit and a corresponding quantity of other eatables, and, of course, drinkables to match.

meal *flour*

—*Louise Amelia Clappe,* The Shirley Letters from the California Mines, 1851–1852. *New York: Alfred A. Knopf, 1949. Originally published in* The Pioneer *magazine, 1854–1855.*

THINK ABOUT THIS

1. What were the two causes of hunger in the camp?

2. Was three dollars a lot to pay for the meal?

Virginia City: Life on Nevada's Comstock Lode

The gold rush of 1849 had taken place on the western, or California, side of the Sierra Nevada. A decade later, prospectors looking for gold on the eastern side of the mountains, in Nevada, came upon the Comstock Lode, one of the richest sources of silver ever

A few years after its birth as a field of shacks and tents, Virginia City, Nevada, boasted a main street with brick houses, hotels, saloons, and stores. But when the nearby silver mines were played out, Virginia City's glory faded as quickly as it had appeared.

found. Overnight a mining town called Virginia City sprang into existence. Reporter J. Ross Browne visited it in March of 1860 and described its wonders for his readers.

ON A SLOPE OF MOUNTAIN speckled with snow, sagebushes, and mounds of upturned earth, without any apparent beginning or end, congruity or regard for the eternal fitness of things, lay outspread the wondrous city of Virginia. Frame shanties, pitched together as if by accident; tents of canvas, or blankets, or brush, or potato-sacks and old shirts with empty whisky-barrels for chimneys; smoky hovels of mud and stone; coyote holes in the mountain side forcibly seized and held by men; pits and shafts with smoke issuing from every crevice; piles of goods and rubbish on craggy points, in the hollows, on the rocks, in the mud, in the snow, everywhere, scattered broadcast in pell-mell confusion, as if the clouds had suddenly burst overhead and rained down the dregs of all the flimsy, rickety, filthy little hovels and rubbish of merchandise that had ever undergone the process of evaporation from the earth since the days of Noah. The intervals of space, which may or may not have been streets, were dotted over with human beings of such sort, variety, and numbers, that the famous ant-hills of Africa were as nothing in comparison.

—*J. Ross Browne,* A Peep at Washoe and Washoe Revisited, *quoted in Russell R. Elliott,* History of Nevada. *Lincoln, NE: University of Nebraska Press, 1987.*

THINK ABOUT THIS

1. What did Browne mean by the word *wondrous* in his description of Virginia City?

2. What was his opinion of the mining town?

3. How did Browne use animal dwellings in his description?

A

GENERAL CIRCULAR

TO ALL

PERSONS OF GOOD CHARACTER,

WHO WISH TO EMIGRATE

TO THE

OREGON TERRITORY,

EMBRACING SOME ACCOUNT OF THE CHARACTER AND
ADVANTAGES OF THE COUNTRY; THE RIGHT
AND THE MEANS AND OPERATIONS BY
WHICH IT IS TO BE SETTLED;—

AND

ALL NECESSARY DIRECTIONS FOR BECOMING

AN EMIGRANT.

Hall J. Kelley, General Agent.

BY ORDER OF THE AMERICAN SOCIETY FOR ENCOURAGING

the SETTLEMENT of the OREGON TERRITORY.

INSTITUTED IN BOSTON, A. D. 1829.

CHARLESTOWN:
PRINTED BY WILLIAM W. WHEILDON.
R. P. & C. WILLIAMS—BOSTON.
1831.

People thinking of going west turned to guidebooks such as this 1831 description of the Oregon Territory. Although most of these books were meant to be helpful, some contained dangerously wrong advice.

Chapter 4

The Overland Trails

EXPLORERS SUCH AS Lewis and Clark and John Charles Frémont blazed the first trails across the West. Mountain Men soon discovered the best routes through the mountains and across the deserts, and they offered their services as guides to pioneers eager to settle in California and in the fertile, well-wooded Oregon country that Lewis and Clark had described.

People who made the trip across the West wrote to friends and relatives back in "the States," sending their letters with returning travelers or on ships that made the months-long voyage from the Pacific coast around South America to New York, Boston, and other Atlantic ports. In these letters they described their journeys. They gave advice on where to camp, where to find water, how to deal with the Native Americans, and what landmarks to use as guides on the trip. Guidebooks for emigrants appeared in the East—including a few that contained dangerously bad advice because their authors had never even seen the places they claimed to be describing!

The best routes to the West received the most use and became well-known trails. The Oregon and California Trail, sometimes called the Oregon Trail, was the main route. It carried travelers and emigrants westward from starting points in Independence, a town in western Missouri. The trail followed the Platte River through what is now Nebraska, then turned slightly north to cross the Rocky Mountains in Wyoming. On the far side of the mountains, in southern Idaho, the trail split in two. The northern branch continued along Idaho's Snake River into Oregon, then along the Columbia River to the valley of the Willamette River, site of most of the early Oregon settlements. The southern branch dipped through Nevada, then climbed the Sierra Nevada range to Sacramento in northern California. Another major trail headed southwest from Missouri, across Kansas and a corner of Colorado to Santa Fe, New Mexico. It was known as the Santa Fe Trail. Farther west another route called the Old Spanish Trail linked Santa Fe with Los Angeles on the coast of southern California.

Missionaries and settlers began moving west along these trails in the 1830s. By the 1840s, the trickle of emigrants had swelled to a flood, and most of them traveled on the Oregon and California Trail. Thousands of men, women, and children made the 2,200-mile journey along the trail, and most of them walked every step of the way. Their wagons were crammed with precious supplies for the journey and for the new lives they planned to begin in the West. Their weary oxen and mules struggled to pull the loads. Only pregnant women, young children, the sick, and the elderly had the luxury of riding in the crowded wagons. Men and older children herded the livestock that went west with the pioneers.

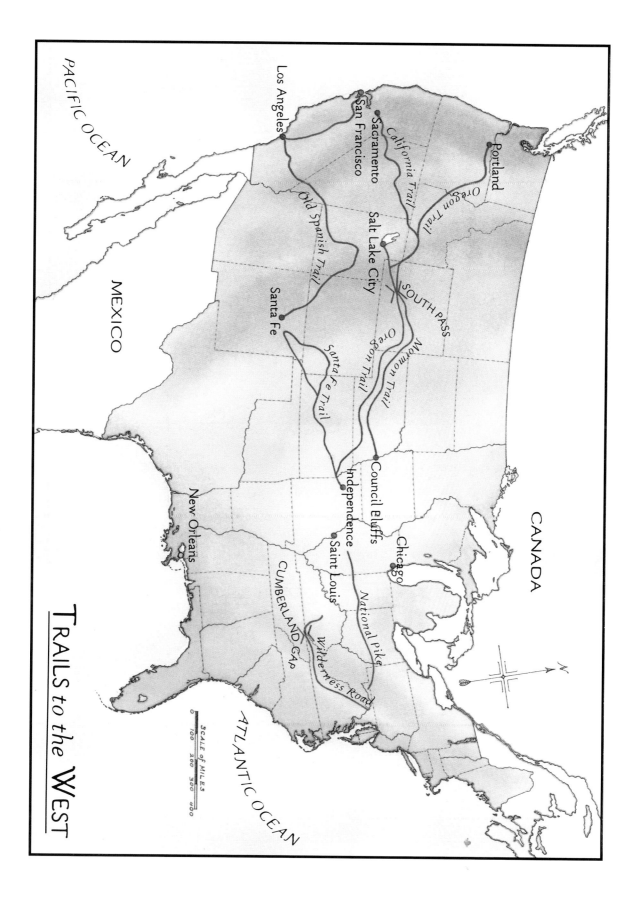

Many people realized that their trip on one of the overland trails was the adventure of a lifetime. They kept diaries of the journey. They wrote about it in letters to their hometowns or in stories to be handed down to their children and grandchildren. Today these writings give us a glimpse of the almost unimaginable challenges faced by the pioneers who opened the West.

A Day on the Oregon Trail Begins

Jesse Applegate caught the "Oregon Fever" of the early 1840s and led one of the first wagon trains to head west from Independence.

Most settlers moved their goods in wagons nicknamed "prairie schooners" because their canvas tops resembled ships' sails. By the time emigrants were being photographed, some western trails had become well-trodden roadways.

The train was part of the Great Migration of 1843, the first year of large-scale travel on the Oregon Trail. In his book about the trip, he told how the wagon train and its herd of cattle started each day.

IT IS 4 O'CLOCK A.M.; the sentinels on duty have discharged their rifles—the signal that the hours of sleep are over—and every wagon and tent is pouring forth its night tenants, and slow-kindling smokes begin largely to rise and float away in the morning air. Sixty men start from the corral, spreading as they make [their way] through the vast herd of cattle and horses that make a semicircle around the encampment, the most distant perhaps two miles away.

The herders pass to the extreme verge and carefully examine for trails beyond, to see that none of the animals have strayed or been stolen during the night. This morning no trails led beyond the outside animals in sight, and by 5 o'clock the herders begin to contract the great moving circle. . . .

From 6 to 7 o'clock is a busy time; breakfast is to be eaten, the tents struck, the wagons loaded and the teams yoked and brought up in readiness to be attached to their respective wagons. All know when, at 7 o'clock, the signal to march sounds, that those not ready to take their proper places in the line of march must fall into the dusty rear for the day. . . .

It is on the stroke of seven; the rush to and fro, the cracking of whips, the loud command to oxen, and what seemed to be the inextricable confusion of the last ten minutes has ceased. Fortunately

"At 7 o'clock, the signal to march sounds . . . those not ready to take their proper places in the line of march must fall into the dusty rear for the day."

every one has been found and every teamster is at his post. The clear notes of a trumpet sound in the front; the leading divisions of the wagon move out of the encampment, and take up the line of march; the rest fall into their places with the precision of clock work, until the spot so lately full of life sinks back into that solitude that seems to reign over the broad plain and rushing river as the caravan draws its lazy length towards the distant El Dorado.

—*Jesse Applegate,* A Day with the Cow Column in 1843. *Chicago: Printed for the Caxton Club, 1934. Originally published in 1868.*

THINK ABOUT THIS

1. What did Applegate think was the dream of the emigrants?

2. What were the herder's responsibilities?

3. Why was it a good idea to be ready to depart promptly at seven o'clock?

"Unladylike Labor": Hauling Wagons over the Rocky Mountains

In 1849 Catherine Haun traveled with her husband from Iowa to the goldfields of California. Years later she wrote an account of the journey that shows the difficulty of moving loaded wagons over rough mountain terrain.

WE HAD NOT TRAVELED many miles in the Black Hills—the beginning of the Rocky Mountains—before we realized that our loads would have to be lightened as the animals were not able to draw the heavily laden wagons over the slippery steep roads. . . .

The roads were rocky and often very steep from this on to the Great Salt Lake—the distance across the Rocky Mountains. Sometimes to keep the wagons from pressing upon the animals in going down grade young pine trees were cut down and after stripping them of all but the top branches they were tied to the front and under the rear axle. The branches dragging upon the ground, or often solid rock, formed a reliable brake. Then again a rope or chain would be tied to the rear of the wagon and every man, woman, and child would be pressed into service to hold the wagon back. At other times a chain or rope would be fastened to the front axle and we climbed up impossible bowlders and pulled with might and main while the men pushed with herculanian strength to get the loaded wagons over some barrier. The animals owing to cramped quarters, were ofen led around the obstacle. Many times the greater part of the day would be consumed in this strenuous and altogether unladylike labor.

And, oh, such pulling, pushing, tugging it was! I used to pity the drivers as well as the oxen and horses—and the rest of us.

"And, oh, such pulling, pushing, tugging it was!"

—*Lillian Schlissel,* Women's Diaries of the Westward Journey.
New York: Schocken Books, 1982.

A Disastrous Shortcut: The Donner-Reed Party

Some travelers on the overland trails met disaster. None found a more dreadful fate than the Donner-Reed party, which left Illinois in 1846, bound for California. They tried to save time by taking a shortcut through the rugged Wasatch Mountains of Utah but lost time instead. When they reached the eastern foothills of the Sierra Nevada, snow had already closed the passes, and the group was forced to spend the winter in cabins left by earlier travelers. They soon ran out of food. As the sick and starving perished one by one, some of the desperate group ate the flesh of the dead. Virginia Reed, who was twelve years old at the time of the ordeal, later wrote about one of the most notorious episodes in the opening of the West. Although Reed carefully avoids saying what she ate, some historians believe that the passage describes the eating of human "meat."

> THE STORMS WOULD OFTEN last ten days at a time, and we would have to cut chips from the logs inside which formed our cabins, in order to start a fire. We could scarcely walk, and the men had hardly enough strength to fetch wood. . . . Poor little children were crying with hunger, and their mothers were crying because they had so little to give their children. We seldom thought of bread, we had been without it so long. Four months of such suffering would fill the bravest hearts with despair. . . .

"We now had nothing to eat but raw hides."

> We now had nothing to eat but raw hides and these were on the roof of the cabin to keep out the snow; when prepared for cooking and boiled they were simply a pot of glue. When the hides were taken off our cabin and we were left without shelter, Mr. Breen gave us a home with his family, and Mrs. Breen prolonged my life by slipping me little bits of meat now and then when she discovered that I could not eat the hide. Death had already claimed many in our party, and it seemed as though relief would never reach us.

—Virginia Reed Murphy, "Across the Plains in the Donner Party (1846)."
Century *magazine*, July 1891.

One of the worst dangers emigrants faced was getting caught on the trail by winter—or even by a freak midsummer snowstorm. Winter's snows brought disaster to the Donner-Reed party and to many other emigrants as well.

THINK ABOUT THIS

What two uses did the snowbound travelers make of animal hides?

Francis Parkman Tells of Trouble along the Trail

Francis Parkman was an unusual traveler on the Oregon Trail—he was a young Bostonian who had just graduated from Harvard University and who planned to become a historian. Parkman journeyed along the Trail in 1846. His goal was not to settle in the West but to study the Indians and emigrants who inhabited it. In this section from his book about the trip, he describes how he and his companions on horseback passed a wagon train that had stopped "for a woman who was in the pangs of childbirth."

THESE WERE THE FIRST EMIGRANTS that we had overtaken, although we had found abundant and melancholy traces of their progress throughout the course of the journey. Sometimes we passed the grave of one who had sickened and died on the way. The earth was usually torn up, and covered thickly with wolf-tracks. Some had escaped this violation. One morning, a piece of plank, standing upright on the summit of a grassy hill, attracted our notice, and riding up to it, we found the following words very roughly traced upon it, apparently with a red-hot iron:—

MARY ELLIS.
DIED MAY 7TH, 1845.
AGED TWO MONTHS. . . .

As we pushed rapidly by the wagons, children's faces were thrust out from the white coverings to look at us; while the care-worn, thin-featured matron, or the buxom girl, seated in front, suspended the knitting on which most of them were engaged, to stare at us with wondering curiosity. By the side of each wagon walked the proprietor, urging on his patient oxen, who shouldered heavily along, inch by inch, on their interminable journey. It was easy to see that fear and dissension prevailed among them; some of the men—but these, with one exception, were bachelors—looked wistfully upon us as we rode lightly and swiftly by, and then impatiently at their own lumbering wagons and heavy-gaited oxen. Others were unwilling to advance at all, until the party they had left behind should have rejoined them. Many were murmuring against the leader they had chosen, and wished to depose him; and this discontent was fomented by some ambitious spirits, who had hopes of succeeding in his place. The women were divided between regrets for the homes they had left and fears of the deserts and savages before them.

—*Francis Parkman,* The Oregon Trail. *Lincoln, NE: University of Nebraska Press, 1994. Originally published in* Knickerbocker *magazine, 1846–1848.*

THINK ABOUT THIS

1. How did the unmarried men in the wagon train react to the sight of Parkman? Why?
2. What were the emigrants arguing about?
3. Why were some of the emigrants critical of the wagon train leader?

The Mormon Migration

In 1847 the Mormons, members of a religion called the Church of Jesus Christ of Latter-Day Saints, began crossing the Great Plains to a colony they founded in Utah. There they hoped to achieve religious freedom and self-government. In the 1850s the Mormons organized migrations without wagons— the travelers hauled their goods in wooden handcarts, something like wheelbarrows. John Chislett, subcaptain of the Fourth Company of the Handcart Migration of 1856, wrote about the sufferings of his group of "Saints" traveling along the Sweetwater River in Wyoming. The mountains were drawing near, the weather was growing colder, food was in short supply, and only faith kept some of the weary marchers on their feet.

"Strong men wept till tears ran freely down their furrowed and sun-burnt cheeks. . . . But help had come too late to save us all."

Thousands of Mormons who could not afford wagons or livestock hauled their possessions across the plains in handcarts. Organized by the Church of Jesus Christ of Latter-Day Saints in the 1850s, the handcart migration significantly boosted the population of the Mormon colony in Utah.

OUR SEVENTEEN POUNDS of clothing and bedding was now altogether insufficient for our comfort. Nearly all suffered more or less at night from cold. Instead of getting up in the morning strong, refreshed, vigorous, and prepared for the hardships of another day of toil, the poor Saints were to be seen crawling out from their tents haggard, benumbed, and showing an utter lack of that vitality so necessary to our success.

Cold weather, scarcity of food, lassitude and fatigue from over-exertion, soon produced their effects. Our old and infirm people began to droop, and they no sooner lost spirit and courage than death's stamp could be traced upon their features. Life went out as smoothly as a lamp ceases to burn when the oil is gone. At first the deaths occurred slowly and irregularly, but in a few days at more frequent intervals, until we soon thought it unusual to leave a camp-ground without burying one or more persons.... Many a father pulled his cart, with his little children on it, until the day preceding his death. I have seen some pull their carts in the morning, give out during the day, and die before the next morning....

[On October 21] just as the sun was sinking beautifully behind the distant hills, on an eminence immediately west of our camp several covered wagons, each drawn by four horses were seen coming towards us. The news ran through the camp like wildfire, and all who were able to leave their beds turned out en masse to see them.... Shouts of joy rent the air; strong men wept till tears ran freely down their furrowed and sun-burnt cheeks, and little children partook of the joy which some of them hardly understood, and fairly danced around with gladness.... But help had come too late to save us all. Nine died that first night.

—*LeRoy R. Hafen and Ann W. Hafen,* Handcarts to Zion: The Story of a Unique Western Migration, 1856–1860, with contemporary journals, accounts, reports; and rosters of members of the ten Handcart Companies. *Spokane, WA: Arthur H. Clark, 1960.*

THINK ABOUT THIS

1. Why were the travelers so worn out?

2. Why did the Mormons rejoice on seeing the newcomers?

Chapter 5

Women and Children in the West

WOMEN AND CHILDREN were part of the opening of the American West from the very beginning. When Lewis and Clark made their historic first crossing of the West, one member of their group was a Shoshone Indian woman named Sacajawea. She worked as hard as any man in the expedition—and did it while caring for her infant son.

Some of the women who left their eastern or midwestern homes for new lives in the West did so willingly and with a sense of excitement. A few were adventurous souls eager to spread their wings on the free-spirited frontier. But many women and youngsters went west because they had no choice. Their husbands or fathers had decided to go, and they had little say in the matter.

Both men and women wrote about the westward journey and about their experiences on the frontier. Men's diaries and letters are generally very different from those of the women. The men tended to write about practical matters: water sources, trouble with the livestock or supplies, how many miles they covered in each day's travel. Women's writings often dealt with more personal details,

A statue on the grounds of the state capitol in Bismarck, North Dakota, honors Sacajawea, the Native American woman who accompanied the Lewis and Clark expedition. She represents all of the women who made the difficult overland journey and shared the work of opening the West.

such as homesickness, fears of the Indians and of wild animals, sorrow for the many who died along the trail, or the hardships of housekeeping in a moving wagon.

The overland trails and life in the West were not all grim. People who crossed the continent as children later remembered marveling at the endless expanses of wildflowers on the prairie and playing happily around the evening campfires. Some pioneer accounts mention festive occasions such as weddings or Independence Day celebrations in the wagon trains. Women's diaries of the Oregon Trail often show pleasure in the wild and magnificent scenery along the way—usually in the early stages of the trip, before exhaustion and hunger set in, food ran short, and the oxen began to go lame.

For most women and children, however, the trip across the West was a time of discomfort and worry—or worse. Many who started the trip did not finish it. Far more people died of disease and accident than were killed by Indians or animals. And when the survivors reached the end of the trail, they were often disappointed by what they found. The first

Missionary Narcissa Whitman is remembered not just as one of the first women pioneers in the West but also as one of the victims of an Indian massacre in eastern Washington in 1847. Cayuse Indians killed the Whitmans and others at their mission because they believed the whites were spreading smallpox among Native Americans.

towns were crude collections of shacks and tents, without churches, schools, or stores. Homesteads were rough patches of land that had to be cleared of trees and rocks. More than one pioneer account tells how a weary woman, at the first sight of what was to be her new western home, buried her head in her hands and wept. Later, though, she rolled up her sleeves and got to work.

A Pioneer Woman Says Goodbye to a Beloved Possession

Narcissa Prentiss Whitman of Massachusetts was one of the first women to cross the continent on what became the Oregon Trail. In 1836 she and her husband, along with another couple, went to Oregon (which then included present-day Washington state) as missionaries to the Indians. Along the way Narcissa Whitman kept a diary in the form of letters to her sister Harriet. Here she describes leaving one of her prized possessions along the trail to lighten the wagon load. Many of the later travelers on the trail had to make the same sad decision. Women's letters and diaries are filled with regrets for treasured pieces of furniture left to decay in the wilderness.

"The custom of the country is to possess nothing and then you will loose nothing while traveling."

DEAR HARRIET, the little trunk you gave me has come with me so far & now I must leave it here alone. Poor little trunk, I am sorry to leave thee. Thou must abide here & no more by this presance remind me of my dear Harriet. Twenty miles below the Falls on Snake River.

This shall be thy place of rest. Farewell little Trunk. I thank thee for thy faithful services & that I have been cheered by thy presance so long. Thus we scatter as we go along.

The hills are so steep [and] rocky that Husband thought it best to lighten the waggon as much as possible & take nothing but the wheels, leaving the box with my trunk. I regret leaving anything that came from home especially that trunk, but it is best. It would have been better for us not to have attempted to bring any baggage whatever, only what [was] necessary to use on the way. It costs so much labor, besides the expense of animals. If I were to make this journey again, I would make quite different preparations. To pack & unpack so many times & cross so many streams, where the packs frequently get wet, requires no small amount of labour, besides the injury done to the articles. Our books what few we have, have been wet several times. In going from Elmira to Williamsport, this trunk fell into the creek and wet all my books & Richard's too, very much. The sleigh box came off, and all of us came near a wetting likewise. The custom of the country is to possess nothing & then you will loose [lose] nothing while traveling. Farewell for the present.

sleigh box
the body of a wagon, fastened on top of a wheeled frame

—*Clifford Merrill Drury, editor,* First White Women over the Rockies: Diaries, Letters, and Biographical Sketches of the Six Women of the Oregon Mission Who Made the Overland Journey in 1836 and 1838. *Glendale, CA: Arthur H. Clark, 1963.*

THINK ABOUT THIS

1. What would Narcissa Whitman have done differently if she were making the journey a second time?
2. What do you think it would be like to "possess nothing"?
3. If you could only bring three possessions with you on your way to a new life, what would you choose? Why?

A Father Catches Oregon Fever

In 1851 a Springfield, Missouri, man named Martin Gay moved to Oregon with his wife and eleven children. One daughter, Martha, was thirteen when the family took to the trail in four wagons. Years later, after a life spent in many frontier settlements in Oregon, Idaho, and Washington, Martha Gay Masterson wrote down her story for her great-nieces.

Two views of the westward journey. The photograph, a primary source, shows an emigrant wagon train struggling through muddy, barren Echo Canyon in northeastern Utah. The painting is a secondary source, a sentimental vision of a pioneer family dominating the landscape.

WE HAD LIVED IN Springfield three years and were very happy and prosperous and the future looked bright. But father got the Western fever. He had talked about Oregon and the Columbia River for many years and wanted to go there. He wanted to take his nine sons where they could get land. . . . Mother was not willing to go. She did not want to undertake the long and dangerous journey with a large family of small children. To cross the plains in those days with ox teams was a fearful undertaking and a tiresome one too. She begged father to give up the notion but he could not. He had received a letter from an old neighbor who had been in Oregon two years. He insisted on father coming West, telling him what a lovely land it was and about the many resources, the genial climate and the rich mines in California.

> *"Lovers, sweethearts and associates were all left behind and we came with our father and mother to Oregon."*

Mother finally reluctantly consented to go. Father at once set about making arrangements for the journey. He told us of his intention and said he wanted us all to go with him to the new country. He told us about the great Pacific Ocean, the Columbia River, the beautiful Willamette Valley, the great forests and the snowcapped mountains. He then explained the hardships and dangers, the sufferings and the dreary long days we would journey on and on before we would reach Oregon. He then asked if we wanted to go. We rather thought we wanted to stay with our school friends and our societies. But children were expected to do as their parents said in those days and father said we must come. Lovers, sweethearts and associates were all left behind and we came with our father and mother to Oregon.

—*Lois Barton, editor,* One Woman's West: Recollections of the Oregon Trail and Settling the Northwest Country by Martha Gay Masterson, 1838–1916. *Eugene, OR: Spencer Butte Press, 1986.*

1. Can you name five reasons why Martha's father wanted to move?
2. Why was Martha's mother reluctant to go to Oregon?
3. How did the children of the family feel about leaving their home?

"I Am Sick and Tired of Work": A California Woman's Letter

The West offered opportunities, but women generally had to work very hard to make those opportunities pay. Mary Jane Megquier and her husband left Maine for California in 1840, leaving their children with relatives. They opened a hotel and managed to earn a living from it, especially after the 1849 gold rush brought people flocking to the area. In a letter dated June 30, 1850, Megquier describes a typical day to her daughter.

"Had I not the constitution of six horses I should [have] been dead long ago."

Dear Daughter

I should like to give you an account of my work if I could do it justice. . . . in the morning the boy gets up and makes a fire by seven o'clock when I get up and make the coffee, then I make the biscuit, then I fry the potatoes, then broil three pounds of steak, and as much liver. . . . at eight the bell rings and they are eating until nine. I do not sit until they are nearly all done. . . . after breakfast I bake six loaves of bread (not very big) then four pies, or a pudding, then we have lamb, for which we have nine dollars a quarter, beef, and pork, baked turnips, beets, potatoes, radishes, salad, and that ever lasting soup, every day, dine at two, for tea we have hash, cold meat bread and butter sauce and some kind of cake and I have cooked every mouthful that has been eaten excepting one day and a half that we were on a steamboat excursion. I make six beds every day and do the washing and ironing you must think I am very busy . . . had I not the constitution of six horses I should [have] been dead long ago but I am going to give up in fall weather or no as I am sick and tired of work.

—*Lillian Schlissel,* Women's Diaries of the Westward Journey.
New York: Schocken Books, 1982.

THINK ABOUT THIS

1. How many meals did Megquier prepare each day? What were these called?
2. Did Megquier mention any recreation? If so, what?

A Texas Cattle Drive

Mary Olivette Taylor was born into a wealthy and prominent family. Her father was a respected doctor in Austin, Texas. In 1885 she married James Bunton, a rancher from a pioneer Texas family. Soon afterward, her husband and his cowhands had to take a herd of cattle north to market along the Chisholm Trail. The new bride insisted on accompanying her husband and became the first woman known to have taken part in a Texas cattle drive. Years later she wrote a book about the adventure.

NATURALLY, AT FIRST, IT was a hardship for me to have to sleep on the ground. Oftentimes I was afraid to go to sleep as I remembered the harrowing tales I had heard of snakes, bugs and crawling and stinging things that infested the woods or prowled around hunting their prey at night. I am ashamed even now to tell how it frightened me when I first heard the snapping and snarling and fighting of the angry, hungry wolf packs as they came closer and closer to our camp at midnight, searching for food. A panacea for my fears as I lay on my pallet at night was turning my face towards the sky, watching the stars. In my last year at school I had studied astronomy and knew quite a few of the constellations and where to look for them. The Pleiades were my favorites.

"Even the early morning was too hot for comfort."

Night after night, I watched them slowly rising through the mellow shade glistening like millions of fireflies tangled in a silver braid.

The first part of the trip was perfect. . . .

There came a day on the trail when even the early morning was too hot for comfort. As the sun rose higher it grew hotter and hotter—the intense heat seemed not only to affect my nerves but to make my head ache and my eyes burn. The horses seemed harder than usual to drive and to keep on the trail. Finally, I was almost in a state of collapse. I wanted to get out of hearing of the lowing of the cattle, and the noisy cowboys slapping their leggings with the quirts, and whistling and calling to the cattle to try to urge the poor leg-weary things and keep them strung out on the trail.

—*Mary Olivette Taylor Bunton,* A Bride on the Old Chisholm Trail in 1886.
San Antonio, TX: Naylor, 1939.

THINK ABOUT THIS

1. What frightened Bunton at night?

2. How did she try to master her fears?

A Letter from a Woman Homesteader

In 1862 President Abraham Lincoln signed the Homestead Act, which opened the Great Plains to settlement. Some historians think that the Homestead Act marked the first time in American history that a single woman could own land in her own right instead of through marriage or inheritance from a male relative. Women homesteaders filed about one-tenth of all the land claims on the Plains. One of them was a single mother named Elinore Pruitt, who in 1909 moved north from Denver to homestead in Wyoming with her daughter, Jerrine. Elinore later married another homesteader, Clyde Stewart. She described her pioneer life in letters to a friend, and these were later published in magazine and book form.

WHEN I READ OF THE HARD TIMES among the Denver poor, I feel like urging them every one to get out and file on land. I am very enthusiastic about women homesteading. It really requires less strength and labor to raise plenty to satisfy a large family than it does to go out to wash, with the added satisfaction of knowing that their job will not be lost to them if they care to keep it. Even if improving the place does go slowly, it is that much done to stay done. Whatever is raised is the homesteader's own, and there is no house-rent to pay. This year Jerrine cut and dropped enough potatoes to raise a ton of fine potatoes. She wanted to try, so we let her, and you will remember that she is but six years old. We had a man to break the ground and cover the potatoes for her and the man irrigated them once. That was all that was done until digging time, when they were ploughed out and Jerrine picked them

"Homesteading is the solution of all poverty's problems."

A U.S. postage stamp commemorates the hundredth anniversary of the Homestead Act. The stamp shows a family, but the Homestead Act also let Elinore Pruitt and many other single women acquire land of their own.

up. Any woman strong enough to go out by the day could have done every bit of the work and put in two or three times that much, and it would have been so much more pleasant than to work so hard in the city and then be on starvation rations in the winter.

To me, homesteading is the solution of all poverty's problems, but I realize that temperament has much to do with success in any undertaking, and persons afraid of coyotes and work and loneliness had better let ranching alone. At the same time, any woman who can stand her own company, can see the beauty of the sunset, loves growing things, and is willing to put in as much time at careful labor as she does over the washtub, will certainly succeed; will have independence, plenty to eat all the time, and a home of her own in the end.

—*Elinore Pruitt Stewart,* Letters of a Woman Homesteader. *Boston: Houghton Mifflin, 1988. Originally published in* Atlantic Monthly *magazine, 1913–1914.*

THINK ABOUT THIS

1. What qualities did Stewart think a woman homesteader should possess?
2. According to Stewart, what were the advantages of homesteading over working as a day laundress in the city?

A ship prepares to leave Liverpool, England, carrying settlers bound for the American West.

Chapter 6

Living and Working on the Land

FOR THE MOST PART, pioneers in the West were a hard-working bunch. Few of them had much leisure. Dr. Benjamin Rush, a Philadelphian who settled in western Pennsylvania, wrote a letter in 1786 to a friend in England, outlining the many things a pioneer on that early frontier had to do to get settled.

"His first object is to build a small cabbin of rough logs for himself and family," wrote Rush. "The floor of this cabbin is earth, the roof is of split logs—the light is received through the door, and, in some instances, thro' a small window made of greased paper. A coarser building adjoining this cabbin affords shelter to a cow, and a pair of poor horses." After building the cabin, the pioneer had to clear a few acres of ground for planting—cutting down the trees and removing the stumps. He had to plant his crop of corn by early summer. Until it ripened in the fall he fed his family by hunting and fishing.

The land rewarded hard work with good yields of crops. Samuel Crabtree, an English settler in the Ohio River valley, wrote to his brother in 1818 that "this is the country for a man to enjoy himself." Crabtree said that he had seen corn plants more than fifteen feet high and "more peaches and apples rotting on the ground than would sink the British fleet." Not all parts of the West were equally suitable for farming, however. The Willamette Valley in Oregon was well watered and had a gentler climate than the Ohio River valley. It proved to be one of the most fertile spots in the West. But many regions of the Southwest were parched and barren. Even the Great Plains, covered with a luxuriant growth of prairie grasses, could not be successfully farmed until people had invented the right tools, such as steel plows to cut through the thick sod and digging equipment to make wells deep enough to reach reliable sources of water.

Farming was the reason why most settlers went west, but it was not the only occupation in the new land. When people gathered in communities, they needed doctors, preachers, teachers, sheriffs, and lawyers, as well as storekeepers and traders. Some of the early pioneers found work guiding the later ones, or helping to transport their goods. And as people settled across the West, new environmental conditions gave rise to new ways to make a living. The open plains of Texas and other western states, for example, supported large herds of cattle, and men were needed to tend those cattle and move them from place to place. The cowboy—one of the enduring symbols of the American West—was born.

Clearing the Land

East Coast merchant John Jacob Astor sent men to establish a fur-trading post on the Pacific Northwest coast in 1810. They were called the Astorians. One of them, Alexander Ross, later wrote of their struggles to build a fort on the site of present-day Astoria, Oregon. None of the Astorians had any experience in felling the massive trees for which the Pacific Northwest became famous.

IT WOULD HAVE MADE A CYNIC SMILE to see this pioneer corps, composed of traders, shopkeepers, voyageurs, and Owhyhees, all ignorant alike in this new walk of life, and the most ignorant of all, the leader. Many of the party had never handled an ax before, and but few of them knew how to use a gun, but necessity, the mother of invention, soon taught us both. . . . In this manner the day would be spent, and often to little purpose: as night often set in before the tree begun with in the morning was half cut down. Indeed, it sometimes required two days, or more, to fell one tree. . . .

There is an art in felling a tree, as well as in planting one; but unfortunately none of us had learned that art, and hours together would be spent in conjectures and discussions: one calling out that it would fall here; another, there; in short, there were as many opinions as there were individuals about it; and, at last, when all hands were assembled to witness the fall, how often were we disappointed! the tree would still stand erect, bidding defiance to our efforts, while every now and then some of the most impatient or fool-hardy would venture to jump on the scaffold and give a blow or two more. Much time was often spent in this desultory manner, before the mighty tree gave way; but it seldom came to the ground. So thick was the forest, and so close the trees together, that in its fall it would often rest its ponderous top on some

Owhyhees
term Ross used for Hawaiian laborers

"Many of the party had never handled an ax before, and but few of them knew how to use a gun, but necessity, the mother of invention, soon taught us both."

other friendly tree; sometimes a number of them would hang together, keeping us in awful suspense, and giving us double labor to extricate the one from the other, and when we had so far succeeded, the removal of the monster stump was the work of days. The tearing up of the roots was equally arduous, although less dangerous: and when this last operation was got through, both tree and stump had to be blown to pieces by gunpowder before either could be removed from the spot.

Nearly two months of this laborious and incessant toil had passed, and we had scarcely yet an acre of ground cleared. In the mean time three of our men were killed by the natives, two more wounded by the falling of trees, and one had his hand blown off by gunpowder.

—*Alexander Ross,* Adventures of the First Settlers on the Oregon or Columbia River, 1810–1813. *Spokane, WA: Arthur H. Clark, 1904.*

THINK ABOUT THIS

1. Which two tools did the Astorians have to master?

2. What were some of the problems they encountered in removing trees?

Drifters and Refugees: A Ferryman on the Snake River

Ben M. Connor came to the West in 1863, in the middle of the Civil War. He was a member of an army unit of mounted soldiers called the Ohio Volunteer Cavalry, assigned to control Indian uprisings on the frontier. He called himself Ben Arnold to hide the fact that he had already deserted from a different military unit. Soon Arnold deserted for a second time and struck out on his own. Near Fort Hall, Idaho, a major trading post along the Oregon Trail,

Arnold worked for a time on a ferry that carried westbound settlers and their goods across the Snake River. In his autobiography he told of a conversation with one such settler.

ONE OF THE GRIZZLED OLD FELLOWS said to me, "Say, young man, I've got a crow to pick with you. Come here." I rode over to his wagon, expecting a berating for some fancied mis-statement. When I neared him he pulled out a jug and a dark looking bowl, and asked, "Do you ever drink?" I told him, "No, I hadn't learned the habit yet," and he nodded. "It's just as well," he said, "you're better off without it." Then after he had helped himself to a drink, continued, "You're the first man who has told us the truth about camping places since we left the Missouri River. We've been robbed at every slough, mudhole, and creek all the way from Missouri." He looked me over meditatively, until I became rather embarrassed by his scrutiny. "You're a truthful lad. I haven't a chick or a child. That's all I have left." He pointed a bony index finger towards his wife. "I lost everything I owned in the war, first pillaged by the Confederates and then by the Yanks. Couldn't sell my land, so just took what little stock and money I had left and started out to look for a place where I can live in peace. I'm bound for Willamette, Oregon, and you'd better come with me."

Sensible of this tribute though I was, I told him I was restless and couldn't stay long in one place. With a far-away look in his eyes and a wistful voice, he said, "I'm sorry. I'm looking for some one who can stay with the old woman and me." The next morning we ferried the whole train of fifty wagons across the Snake River.

—*Lewis F. Crawford,* The Exploits of Ben Arnold: Indian Fighter, Gold Miner, Cowboy, Hunter, and Army Scout. *Norman, OK: University of Oklahoma Press, 1999. Originally published as* Rekindling Camp Fires, *1926.*

The Chinese Come to Gold Mountain

Americans and Europeans came to the West from the eastern part of the United States. Some people, however, came from the other direction—from across the Pacific Ocean. During the middle of the nineteenth century, famine and other troubles in China led many Chinese men to set out for California. They called the new land "Gold Mountain" because they had heard that gold could be found in the Sierra Nevada range. They arrived in San Francisco

Chinese miners in California in the 1850s. Dreams of wealth brought the Chinese to the West, which they called "Gold Mountain." Few found much gold, but many built new lives in America, overcoming loneliness and racial prejudice.

and set out from there for the goldfields. Here is how one Cau-
casian visitor to the mining camps described the new arrivals.

CROWDS OF CHINAMEN were also to be seen, bound for the diggings,
under gigantic basket-hats, each man with a bamboo laid across his
shoulder, from each end of which was suspended a higgledy-piggledy
collection of mining tools, Chinese baskets and boxes, immense boots
and a variety of Chinese "fixins" which no one but a Chinaman could
tell the use of, all speaking at once, gabbling and chattering their
horrid jargon, and producing a noise like that of a flock of geese.

—*J. B. Borthwick*, The Gold-Hunters: A First-Hand Picture of Life in California
Mining Camps in the Early Fifties. *New York: Outing Publishing Co., 1917.*

THINK ABOUT THIS

1. How would you describe the speaker's attitude toward the Chinese
   immigrants?
2. Can you imagine how the Chinese felt when they arrived in America?

The Cowboy: Villain or Hero?

The western frontier had room for all kinds of people, good and
bad alike. Some people saw the frontier as a dangerous place full of
violent individuals who could not get along in civilized society.
Others believed that the frontier brought out the best qualities in
human nature: strength, bravery, and generosity. Those very different views appear in two newspaper descriptions of cowboys from
the 1880s.

IT IS POSSIBLE THAT THERE is not a wilder or more lawless set of men in any country that pretends to be civilized than the gangs of semi-nomads that live in some of our frontier States and Territories and are referred to . . . as "the cow boys." Many of them have emigrated from our States in order to escape the penalty of their crimes, and it is extremely doubtful whether there is one in their number who is not guilty of a penitentiary offense, while most of them merit the gallows. They are supposed to be herdsmen employed to watch vast herds of cattle, but they might more properly be known under any name that means desperate criminal. They roam about in sparsely settled villages with revolvers, pistols and knives

Cold Morning on the Range was painted around 1904 by Frederic Remington, who produced many famous images of the Old West. Popular fiction and art helped make the cowboy into a new kind of American hero.

in their belts, attacking every peacable citizen met with. Now and then they take part in a dance, the sound of the music frequently being deadened by the crack of their pistols, and the hoe-down only being interrupted long enough to drag out the dead and wounded. [*Las Vegas Optic,* New Mexico, June 28, 1881]

WE DEEM IT HARDLY NECESSARY to say in the next place that the cowboy is a fearless animal. A man wanting in courage would be as much out of place in a cow-camp, as a fish would be on dry land. Indeed the life he is daily compelled to lead calls for the existence of the highest degree of cool calculating courage. As a natural consequence of this courage, he is neither quarrelsome nor a bully. As another consequence to possessing true manly courage, the cowboy is as chivalrous as the famed knights of old. Rough he may be, and it may be that he is not a master in ball room etiquette, but no set of men have loftier reverence for women and no set of men would risk more in the defence of their person or their honor. [*Texas Live Stock Journal,* 1882]

—*Richard W. Slatta,* Cowboys of the Americas.
New Haven, CT: Yale University Press, 1990.

THINK ABOUT THIS

1. According to the first writer, why did many of the cowboys go to the West?
2. The second writer was convinced that the cowboys were courageous and chivalrous. Why?
3. Which writer do you think is correct?

Chapter 7

Building the New West

INDEPENDENCE WAS MORE than the name of a town at the start of the Oregon Trail. It was also a quality that pioneers needed. People who moved beyond the settled lands spent a lot of time alone, or with only their families for company. They had to be able to do things and make things for themselves because they could not count on finding a doctor, a tailor, a shoemaker, or a store on the frontier.

One lasting image of the American West is of the rugged loner who was more at home in the wide-open spaces than in the crowded cities and snug towns of the East. True, the frontier attracted strong individualists like the Mountain Men. But very few frontierspeople really wanted to be alone all the time. Even the hardy and independent fur trappers often worked in teams, and every year they gathered in a huge weeklong camp in the mountains to sell their furs to traders from Saint Louis—and to drink, swap tales, and visit with each other.

People and families moving west often traveled with others not just for company but for protection from Indians and other

By the mid-1840s, parts of Oregon's Willamette Valley were already well settled. This view of Oregon City contrasts the "civilization" of one riverbank with the undeveloped land, populated by Indians, on the other bank.

possible dangers along the way. It was natural for people who traveled together to settle near one another, or near friends and family members who had already gone west. In this way communities began to form. Even when each family lived on its own spreading ranch or farm, some central settlement took shape as soon as settlers got around to building a store, church, or school. Settlements became villages, and villages became towns, and some towns—especially those located on rivers or coastal ports or near major resources such as mines—grew into cities. In a surprisingly short time the once-wild West was crisscrossed with trails and roads linking a network of communities, and frontier territories became settled states.

Communication and transportation improved rapidly in the later years of the opening of the West. By 1860 several companies, including the famed Pony Express, were carrying goods and mail across the West along scheduled routes. The following year the first transcontinental telegraph line was completed, and the country's two coasts could communicate instantly. The Civil War interrupted development in the West during the early 1860s, but after the war people once again began moving westward in wagon trains and stagecoaches. By 1869 two railroad companies had finished laying the track for the first transcontinental railway. Trains allowed passengers to travel in four days over a distance that had taken the first Oregon Trail emigrants five months to cover.

The 1860s and 1870s saw the settling of the Great Plains, the Southwest, and Texas. The 1880s brought the last major "land rush" of the West when Oklahoma, once set aside as Indian Territory, was opened to settlement. Cattle ranching became an important industry across large stretches of the West. Railways multiplied, carrying cattle and other western goods such as timber and grain to ports and markets. Americans had succeeded in taming their western frontier. Now they were shaping new cities, states, and industries.

Working Together: House-Raising in the Ohio River Valley

One of many frontier settlers who wrote books to guide other settlers was John Knight, who came from England to the Ohio River valley in the early nineteenth century. His handbook tells how people on the frontier pitched in to help each other build houses—and communities.

Working together was a way of life for Americans on the frontier. Many illustrations of pioneer life emphasize neighborliness and cooperation. This image also shows that building was considered men's work and cooking women's work.

IN THE SETTLEMENT of a community, there are many things to be done, which require the united strength of many; this money cannot purchase: but that kind and generous feeling, which men (not rendered callous by wealth or poverty) have for each other, comes to their relief. The neighbors, (even unsolicited) appoint a day, when as a frolic, they shall (for instance,) build the new settler a house.—On the morning appointed, they assemble; and divide themselves into parties: one party cuts down the trees; another lops them and cuts them into proper lengths; a third, (with horses or oxen) drag them to the intended spot; another party make shingles for the roof; and at night all the materials are on the spot: and the night of the next day, the family sleep in their new habitation.—No payment is expected, nor would be received: it is considered a duty; and lays him under obligation, to assist the next settler. But this cooperation of labour is not confined to new settlers; it occurs frequently, in the course of a year, amongst the old settlers, with whom it is a bond of amity and social intercourse; and in no part of the world, is good neighbourship, in greater perfection, than in America.

—*John Knight,* The Emigrants Best Instructor, or, the most Recent and Important Information respecting the United States of America, selected from the Works of the latest Travellers in that Country. *Manchester, England: M. Wilson, 1818.*

THINK ABOUT THIS

How was a new settler expected to repay his neighbors' help in house-raising?

One City's Growth: Spokane, Washington

Some people who had come west in the early days of settlement were amazed by the changes that occurred during their lifetimes. Martha Gay Masterson, who had traveled the Oregon Trail as a teenager in 1851, lived in Spokane, Washington, from 1886 to 1889. Her first home in the West had been a crude settlement of log

The rapid growth of Spokane, Washington, eventually drove Martha Gay Masterson and her husband to leave the city for somewhere less hectic and crowded. Spokane became the unofficial capital of a region known as the "Inland Empire," the wheat-growing territory of eastern Washington and Oregon and western Idaho.

cabins and muddy trails, but her description of Spokane reveals a very different kind of West.

THE YEARS GO BY and three had passed since our coming to this thrifty little town. What a change! Magnificent buildings on every side. Business was rushing. Crowded streets. Throngs of people hurrying here and there. Electric cars and city coaches filled with stylish ladies and professional gentlemen looking about them for locations. From 5,000, it now numbered 25,000 inhabitants and still they came. Railroads too were coming in on every side. It was now a center, a city of magic, a beautiful city . . . .

"From 5,000, it now numbered 25,000 inhabitants and still they came."

We must give up our house on Front Street. Lots were in demand on the river bank for mills and factories. We went toward the heights to Lincoln Street. We had a fine view of the city from our upper verandah, and we liked the situation and neighborhood much better. . . .

We had lived a year on Lincoln Street and were being crowded out again by business blocks. A large, three-story cold storage building loomed up at our front door and shut off our nice view. Some of our neighbors moved away, and we thought of going to Pend Oreille Lake in northern Idaho. I was sorry to leave my neighbors.

—*Lois Barton, editor,* One Woman's West: Recollections of the Oregon Trail and Settling the Northwest Country by Martha Gay Masterson, 1838–1916. *Eugene, OR: Spencer Butte Press, 1986.*

Celebrating Statehood

The western lands entered the United States in stages. First, the United States had to annex the land, acquiring it by purchase, conquest, or treaty from other countries that claimed it and from the Indians that occupied it. Then the U.S. Congress divided the newly acquired land into units called territories and assigned a governor to each territory. A territory also had a legislature through which the local people governed themselves, but the governor had greater authority. When a territory had enough inhabitants it could ask to become a state. The territorial legislature had to write a state constitution and send it to Congress for approval. Once Congress approved the constitution, the territory achieved statehood. Its citizens could elect their own governor and consider themselves fully part of the American nation. Becoming a state was a momentous occasion in every western territory. Rebecca Howell Mace, a widow in the small town of Kanab, Utah, wrote a newspaper article about how Kanab celebrated Utah's entry into the Union on January 4, 1896.

ON THE 6TH—MONDAY, . . . the new State . . . was inaugurated, the day being set apart as a holiday to be remembered as such forever. It was enjoyed to the utmost.

Guns were fired at daybreak. 10:00 a procession was formed, led by the Band of Home Guards—followed by citizens, also a juvenile corps, or Bell Brigade.

At two o'clock the citizens met in the Social Hall and partook of a

"It will be a day long to be remembered."

Pic Nic Dinner, then followed speech and song, closing the day with a grand Inaugural Ball.

The day was all that could be desired. The weather was pleasant and all enjoyed themselves, there was nothing to mar the occasion, and it will be a day long to be remembered by the inhabitants of Kanab both old and young.

—*Dean L. May,* Utah: A People's History. *Salt Lake City: University of Utah Press, 1987.*

San Francisco's "China Boys"

The West was a multicultural world. In addition to the Native American population and the white and black settlers from the eastern states, the West became home to emigrants from Asia. The first to arrive were the Chinese, who established a community in San Francisco, California, that still thrives today. Although Asian immigrants met with racist hostility from some white Americans and with laws that kept them from becoming full citizens, many of them considered America their home. They made every effort to become part of it, as this letter, written by representatives of the Chinese community in San Francisco, shows. The letter was addressed to the city's mayor after he invited them to take part in a parade being planned in honor of President Zachary Taylor, who had just died. The presence of the Chinese paraders, with colorful silk clothing and banners, was such a hit that they were included in every procession in San Francisco after that time.

SAN FRANCISCO, AUGUST 30, 1850

To Hon. John W. Geary, Mayor of the City of San Francisco

Sir: The "China Boys" wish to thank you for the kind mark of attention you bestowed on them in extending to them an invitation to join with the citizens of San Francisco in doing honor to the memory of the late president of the United States, Gen. Zachary Taylor. The China Boys feel proud of the distinction you have shown them, and will always endeavor to merit your good opinion and the good opinion of the citizens of their adopted country. The China Boys are fully sensible of the great loss this country has sustained in the death of its chieftain and ruler, and mourn with you in sorrow. Strangers as they are among you, they kindly appreciate the many kindnesses received at your hands, and again beg leave, with grateful hearts, to thank you.

    Ah-Sing

    A-He

    In behalf of the China Boys.

—*Charles Caldwell Dobie,* San Francisco's Chinatown. *New York: Appleton-Century, 1939.*

THINK ABOUT THIS

1. How would you describe the tone of the letter?
2. What do you think it was like to be a member of a minority community in the Old West? What problems did minorities encounter?

A Black Cowboy in Texas

African Americans were part of the West, too—from early adventurers such as James Beckwourth to the liberated slaves who migrated westward and struggled to establish communities on the Great Plains after the Civil War. Ben Kinchlow was born in 1846 to a slave in Texas. His mother was freed the next year but took her two boys across the border to Mexico, fearing they might be forced into slavery if they stayed in Texas. Ben grew up in Matamoros, across the Río Grande from Brownsville, Texas. After slavery ended in the United States, he went north to Texas and became a cowboy. Years later his life story was recorded for posterity.

"We had to wear our guns all the time."

I USED TO GET four-bits a head for every Maverick I roped out and branded. You know people couldn't get out to brand up all their stock and after the calves were a year old, they were considered Mavericks. They had quit their mother, then. Yes, instead of branding 'em up for myself, I got four-bits a head to make the other man rich. Well, I didn't want nothin' them days but a pair of boots, a six-shooter, and a big hat. . . . Anyhow, we had a pretty good outfit. We could rope any bull or cow that come along. I wore these regular old Mexkin [Mexican] spurs with a sort of short shank but a big rowel. I carried a .45 six-shooter. We had to wear our guns all the time and we tucked them down in our belts under our leggings. We carried guns mostly for the Indians, but lots of times they was dirt done that the Indians didn't do.

—Ben Kinchlow, recorded as U.S. Works Progress Administration, Federal Writers Project, American Life Histories; "Ben Kinchlow: Range Lore and Negro Cowboy Reminiscences before and after 1875." Interview by Florence Angermiller, Library of Congress, 1936–1940.

A cowboy's life held the promise of excitement and romance for many young men. When Ben Kinchlow started out, he didn't aspire to anything more than "a good pair of boots, a six-shooter, and a big hat."

THINK ABOUT THIS

1. What do you think Kinchlow meant when he said there was "dirt done" on the range by people other than the Indians? Why did he and the other cowboys carry guns?

2. How did Kinchlow define a "Maverick"?

Black Hawk, chief of the Sauk people of Illinois, fought hard to preserve his people's lands but ended up spending his final days on a reservation.

Chapter 8

The Fate of the Native Americans

WHOLE NATIONS HAVE melted away like balls of snow before the sun," said Dragging Canoe, son of a Cherokee chief in the Ohio River valley in 1775. He was talking about the Indian nations that had disappeared from eastern North America. Many Indians had died of sicknesses they caught from the whites. Others had been killed in fighting or pushed off their land by Europeans. Dragging Canoe went on to remind his fellow Cherokee that whites eventually broke every treaty they had signed with the Indians. He called the whites a "greedy host" who kept advancing onto lands they had promised to leave for the Indians. "Such treaties may be all right for men too old to hunt or fight," the Cherokee concluded. "As for me, I have my young warriors about me. We will have our lands."

The opening of the West is a heroic chapter in American history, filled with examples of courage, endurance, and imagination. It is also a shameful chapter, with dark stories of betrayal and bloodshed. From the early days of the colonial era to the final settling of the Great Plains, violence between whites and Native

Americans simmered steadily, sometimes flaming up into the conflicts known as "the Indian wars." The bloodshed was on both sides—whites and Indians committed violent acts and massacred innocent women and children as well as warriors. The betrayal, however, was all on the part of the whites. Europeans and then Americans repeatedly cheated the Indians and broke the agreements they had made with them.

During the early part of the nineteenth century, many of the remaining Indians east of the Mississippi River were forced to move west of the river. The defeated Cherokee were among them. In the West, the U.S. government adopted a policy of moving the Indians to tracts of land called reservations. The government expected that in time it could make the Indians speak English, become Christian, and adopt American ways such as farming. A few white Americans spoke out against the unjust treatment of the native peoples. In 1881 Helen Hunt Jackson published *A Century of Dishonor,* a bitter criticism of American policy toward the Indians. Voices

Indians in Oklahoma, photographed in 1890, after the Great Plains had been opened to white settlement and Native Americans were confined to reservations

like hers were drowned out, however, in the clamor for land and the calls to wipe out the Indian threat.

Individual encounters between pioneers and Indians were often peaceful, even friendly. Many a woman's diary from the Oregon Trail tells of her fear when she saw her first wild Indians. Mothers were certain that howling savages would descend upon the camps at night and slaughter the children in their beds. By the end of the trail, however, pioneer women were calmly trading needles and mirrors to Indians for moccasins and fresh fish, while their children fearlessly explored the Indian camps they passed and sometimes played with Indian children. But in spite of many friendly meetings and exchanges, there was no real peace between whites and Indians in the West until the U.S. Army had beaten down the last stubborn struggles of people fighting to keep control of their homelands.

The words that follow are from speeches by Indian leaders. Many of these men, such as Tecumseh, had reputations as great speech makers whose words stirred their audiences. The problem with all such speeches is that the Indians did not write them down. White listeners wrote them down, sometimes hours or even days later. And because Indians generally spoke in their own languages, the recorded words had been translated into English by either Indian or white interpreters. In short, there is no way to know whether the speeches that have passed down to us are what the chieftains really said. But if the records of these Indians' thoughts are not accurate to the last word, they do reflect the anger and sorrow that Native American leaders felt when they saw their world coming to an end.

Tecumseh Calls for War on the Whites

Tecumseh was a chieftain and war leader of the Shawnee people, who fought to keep whites out of the Ohio River valley in the late seventeenth and early eighteenth centuries. During the War of 1812 Tecumseh allied himself with the British against the Americans. He was killed by American troops in Canada in 1813. Two years earlier he had spoken these passionate words to the Creek people, urging them to join with other tribes to fight the white settlers.

"Burn their houses, destroy their stock!"

LET THE WHITE RACE PERISH! They seize your land, they corrupt your women, they trample on the grass of your dead. Back whence they came, upon a trail of blood, they must be driven. Back, back, aye, into the great waters whose accursed waves brought them to our shores. Burn their houses, destroy their stock! The red man owns the country and the palefaces must never enjoy it. War now, war forever! War upon the living, war upon the dead. Dig their bones from the grave. Our country must give no rest to a white man's bones.

—*Glenn Tucker, Tecumseh:* Vision of Glory. *New York: Russell and Russell, 1973.*

THINK ABOUT THIS

What are the "great waters" that Tecumseh mentions? Why were their waves "accursed"?

Black Hawk Foresees the Indians' Future

Like Tecumseh, Black Hawk, a chieftain of the Sauk people in Illinois, fought against settlers and sided with the British in the War of 1812. After the war, most of the Sauk moved west of the Mississippi, giving up their lands to the white settlers. But Black Hawk and his followers clashed with the army in the Black Hawk war, a short but savage conflict in 1832. After surrendering to General Joseph M. Street with these words, Black Hawk was forced to spend the rest of his life on a reservation in Iowa.

"They ought to be ashamed . . ."

HE IS NOW A PRISONER to the white man, but he can stand the torture. He is not afraid of death. He is no coward—Black Hawk is an Indian. He has done nothing of which an Indian need be ashamed. He has fought the battles of his country against the white man, who came year after year to cheat his people and take away their lands. You know the cause of our making war. It is known to all white men. They ought to be ashamed of it. The white men despise the Indians and drive them from their homes. But the Indians are not deceitful. Indians do not steal. Black Hawk is satisfied. He will go to the world of spirits contented. He has done his duty. His Father will meet and reward him. The white men do not scalp the head, but they do worse—they poison the heart. It is not pure with them. His countrymen will not be scalped, but they will in a few years become like the white man, so that you cannot hurt them; and there must be, as in the white settlements, as many men, to take care of them and keep them in order. Farewell to my nation! Farewell to Black Hawk!

—Alexander R. Fulton, The Red Men of Iowa. *Des Moines, IA: Mills and Company, 1882.*

1. According to Black Hawk, how were the Indians different from the whites?

2. What kind of life does Black Hawk foresee for his people? What would his own fate be?

3. What effect do you think Black Hawk had on his listeners by speaking in the third person?

Numaga Warns against Fighting a Doomed War

In 1861, in Owens Valley in eastern California, fighting broke out between the white miners and settlers and the local Paiute Indians. The Paiute called for help from Paiute groups living in Nevada, but the Nevada Paiute had been fighting with whites in their own territory. They had learned that fighting would not help the Indians. Numaga, a chieftain of the Nevada Paiute, advised the Owens Valley Indians not to go to war.

YOU WOULD MAKE WAR upon the whites. I ask you to pause and reflect. The white men are like the stars over your heads. You have wrongs, great wrongs that rise up like those mountains before you; but can you from the mountain tops reach and blot out those stars? Your enemies are like the sands in the bed of your rivers; when taken away they only give place for more to come and settle there. Could you defeat the whites in Nevada, from over the mountains in California would come to help them an army of white men that would cover your country like a blanket. What hope is there for the Pah-Ute? From

"Your enemies are like the sands in the bed of your rivers."

where is to come your guns, your powder, your lead, your dried meats to live upon, and hay to feed your ponies while you carry on this war? Your enemies have all these things, more than they can use. They will come like the sand in a whirlwind and drive you from your homes. You will be forced among the barren rocks of the north, where your ponies will die; where you will see the women and old men starve, and listen to the cries of your children for food. I love my people; let them live, and when their spirits shall be called to the Great Camp in the southern sky, let their bones rest where their fathers were buried.

—*Roger D. McGrath,* Gunfighters, Highwaymen & Vigilantes: Violence on the Frontier. *Berkeley, CA: University of California Press, 1984.*

THINK ABOUT THIS

1. Why did Numaga think the whites would win in the end?
2. Do you think Numaga was an effective speaker? To what two aspects of nature did Numaga compare the whites in order to make his point?

The Chieftain and the General

Two worlds collided in 1867 at Fort Hays, Kansas. There Satanta, a chieftain of the Kiowa people, and General Winfield Scott Hancock of the U.S. Army exchanged words about the construction of a railroad across the Great Plains. Henry Morton Stanley, a British journalist who would become famous as an explorer of Central Africa, was present and wrote about the incident years later. Satanta spoke first.

A photo of Kiowa chief Satanta taken in the late 1860s or early 1870s. Although he had already lost the fight to hold on to his ancestral lands, Satanta proudly poses with a bow and arrow.

I want the Great Father at Washington and all the soldiers and troops to go slowly. I don't want the prairies and country to be bloody. I don't want war at all. I want peace. As for the Kiowas talking war, I don't know anything about it. Nor do I know anything about the Comanches, Cheyennes, and Sioux talking about war. The Cheyennes, Kiowas, and Comanches are poor. They are all of the same colour. They are all red men. This country here is old, and it all belongs to them. You are cutting off the timber, and now the country is of no account at all. I don't mean anything bad by what I say. I have nothing bad hidden in my breast at all; everything is all right. I had heard that there were many troops coming out to this country to whip the Cheyennes, and that is the reason we were afraid and went away. The Cheyennes, Arapahoes, and Kiowas heard that there were troops coming out to this country; so did the Comanches and Apaches; but did not know whether the soldiers were coming for peace or for war. [Satanta, Kiowa chief]

"I don't want war at all. I want peace."

THE WHITE MEN ARE COMING out here so fast that nothing can stop them—coming from the east and coming from the west, like a prairie on fire in a high wind. The reason of it is because the whites are a great people, and they are spreading out and we cannot help it. Those on one sea in the west want to communicate with another sea in the east, and that is the reason they are building these waggon roads, and railroads and telegraphs. The Great Father had a council with these tribes, and asked their permission to run roads through here, and you and the others gave your permission. That treaty was made at the mouth of the Little Arkansas; and last fall it was signed again, and it is too late to reconsider it now. I don't know where the railroad is going to run. It may run on the Smoky Hill, and they may find a better road on this line. At any rate, if the railroad comes here, I cannot help it, and you have already given your assent to it. [General Winfield Scott Hancock]

"The white men are coming out here so fast that nothing can stop them . . . like a prairie on fire in a high wind."

—Henry Morton Stanley, My Early Travels and Adventures in America and Asia. *Lincoln, NE: University of Nebraska Press, 1982. Originally published in 1895.*

THINK ABOUT THIS

1. How would you describe Santanta's tone? Do you think he was trying to please the general, or was he expressing anger?
2. What was General Hancock's argument?

Chief Joseph Gives Up the Fight

One of the last chieftains to surrender to the whites was Chief Joseph of the Nez Perce, a Pacific Northwest tribe. When the U.S. government ordered the Nez Perce of eastern Oregon to move onto a reservation in Idaho, fighting broke out. Joseph had not wanted to fight, and he had not launched the Indian attack, but when the other chiefs were killed, he carried on the fight. In a final desperate

Chief Joseph, around 1890

effort to escape from the U. S. Army, he led his surviving followers on a cold, hungry, and miserable trek through the Rocky Mountains. Rather than see them all die, he surrendered to the army on October 5, 1877, in the Bear Paw Mountains of Montana.

I AM TIRED OF FIGHTING. Our chiefs are killed. Looking Glass is dead. The old men are all killed. It is the young men who say yes or no. He who led the young men is dead. It is cold and we have no blankets. The little children are freezing to death. My people, some of them, have run away into the hills and have no blankets, no food; no one knows where they are, perhaps freezing to death. I want time to look for my children and see how many of them I can find. Maybe I shall find them among the dead. Hear me, my chiefs, I am tired; my heart is sick and sad. From where the sun now stands, I will fight no more forever.

—McWhorter, Lucullus Virgil, Hear Me, My Chiefs. Caldwell, ID: Caxton, 1952.

Glossary

annex to add new land to a nation or territory

colonize to establish settlers from a country in a place that is not part of that country

conquistadors Spanish military conquerors who were also explorers

emigrant one who emigrates, or leaves his or her homeland to live somewhere else

immigrant one who immigrates, or enters a country from somewhere else

militia a group of citizens organized for military service

missionary one who works to convert others to his or her religion

prehistoric before people began to record history in written records

reservations land set aside by the U.S. government for Native Americans

transcontinental reaching from one side of the continent to the other

Time Line

1803
President Thomas Jefferson makes Louisiana Purchase, extending U.S. territory to the Rocky Mountains.

1763
Great Britain wins part of France's territory in North America at end of French and Indian War (Seven Years' War in Europe). Britain issues the Proclamation of 1763 to prevent American colonists from settling west of the Appalachian Mountains.

1818
Great Britain and the United States agree to share the region known as Oregon.

1787
Ship captain Robert Gray is the first American to land on the Pacific coast of Oregon.

1804–06
Meriwether Lewis and William Clark lead an American expedition from the Mississippi River to the Oregon coast and back.

1843
The first large wagon train carries emigrants to Oregon and California.

1846

The United States adds Texas to its territory. The War with Mexico begins.

1848

After a two-year war with Mexico, the United States acquires California and the Southwest in the Treaty of Guadalupe Hidalgo. The California Gold Rush begins.

1893

The U.S. Census Bureau announces that the American frontier had closed in 1880.

1847

The first Mormons arrive in Utah.

1862

President Abraham Lincoln signs the Homestead Act, opening the Great Plains to settlement.

1869

The first transcontinental railway line across the United States is completed. John Wesley Powell leads the first expedition through the Grand Canyon of the Colorado River.

To Find Out More

BOOKS

Allen, John Logan. *Jedediah Smith and the Mountain Men of the American West.* New York: Chelsea House, 1991.

Alter, Judith. *Growing Up in the Old West.* New York: Franklin Watts, 1989.

Altman, Linda Jacobs. *The California Gold Rush in American History.* Springfield, NJ: Enslow, 1997.

Bial, Raymond. *Frontier Home.* Boston: Houghton Mifflin, 1993.

Blumberg, Rhoda. *The Great American Gold Rush.* New York: Bradbury Press, 1989.

Butruille, Susan G. *Women's Voices from the Oregon Trail.* Boise, ID: Tamarack Books, 1993.

Cavan, Seamus. *Lewis and Clark and the Route to the Pacific.* New York: Chelsea House, 1991.

Duncan, Dayton. *People of the West.* Boston: Little, Brown, 1996.

Fisher, Leonard. *The Oregon Trail.* New York: Holiday House, 1990.

Freedman, Russell. *Children of the Wild West.* New York: Clarion Books, 1983.

Murdoch, David Hamilton. *North American Indian.* New York: Dorling Kindersley, 2000.

Press, Petra. *A Multicultural Portrait of the Move West.* New York: Marshall Cavendish, 1994.

Schlissel, Lillian. *The Way West: Journal of a Pioneer Woman.* New York: Simon & Schuster Books for Young Readers, 1993.

Stefoff, Rebecca. *Children of the Westward Trail.* Brookfield, CT: Millbrook Press, 1996.

———. *The Oregon Trail in American History.* Springfield, NJ: Enslow, 1997.

———. *Women Pioneers.* New York: Facts On File, 1995.

WEBSITES

The websites listed here were in existence in 2000–2001 when this book was being written. Their names or locations may have changed since then.

In general, when using the Internet to do research on a history topic, you should use caution. You will find numerous websites that are very attractive to look at and appear to be professional in format. Proceed with caution, however. Many, even the best ones, contain errors. Some websites even insert disclaimers or warnings about mistakes that may have made their way onto the site. In the case of primary sources, the builders of the website often transcribe previously published material, good or bad, accurate or inaccurate. Therefore, you have to judge the content of *all* websites. This requires a critical eye.

A good rule for using the Internet as a resource is always to compare what you find in websites to several other sources such as librarian- or teacher-recommended reference works and major works of scholarship. By doing this, you will discover the myriad versions of history that exist.

www.pbs.org/weta/thewest is the home page of New Perspectives on the West, based on the eight-part public television series "The West."

www.americanwest.com has information about many aspects of the West, including westward expansion and Native Americans, as well as links to dozens of other pages.

www.pbs.org/opb/oregontrail is the home page of "In Search of the Oregon Trail," an on-line resource based on the public television series "The Oregon Trail."

www.teleport.com/~eotic connects to The End of the Oregon Trail Interpretive Center in Oregon City, Oregon, with material for students and teachers on the westward migration.

www.museumca.org/goldrush, maintained by the Oakland Museum of California, is a reference site for the Gold Rush of 1849.

Index

Page numbers for illustrations are in boldface

Rebecca Stefoff has written a number of books about the exploration and settling of the American West, including several of the volumes in Marshall Cavendish's North American Historical Atlases series. She lives in Portland, Oregon, at the end of the trail that so many men, women, and children followed across the continent during the opening of the West.